STORIES AND BALLADS
OF THE FAR PAST

STORIES AND BALLADS
OF THE FAR PAST

TRANSLATED FROM THE NORSE
(ICELANDIC AND FAROESE)
WITH INTRODUCTIONS AND NOTES

BY

N. KERSHAW

CAMBRIDGE
AT THE UNIVERSITY PRESS
1921

CAMBRIDGE UNIVERSITY PRESS
Cambridge, New York, Melbourne, Madrid, Cape Town,
Singapore, São Paulo, Delhi, Tokyo, Mexico City

Cambridge University Press
The Edinburgh Building, Cambridge CB2 8RU, UK

Published in the United States of America by
Cambridge University Press, New York

www.cambridge.org
Information on this title: www.cambridge.org/9781107600454

First published 1921
First paperback edition 2011

A catalogue record for this publication is available from the British Library

ISBN 978-1-107-60045-4 Paperback

Preface

VERY few of the *Fornaldar Sögur Northrlanda* have hitherto been translated into English. The *Völsungasaga* is of course well known, but with this exception the 'Stories of Icelanders,' and the 'Stories of the Kings of Norway' are probably the only sagas familiar to the majority of English readers. Of the four sagas contained in this volume only one— the *Tháttr of Sörli*—has appeared in English before, though the poetry which they contain has frequently been translated, from the time of Hickes's *Thesaurus* (1705). So far as I am aware no version of any of the Faroese ballads has appeared in English. Out of the great number which were collected during the 18th and 19th centuries I have chosen a few which deal with the same stories as the sagas translated here; and for purposes of comparison I have added a short extract from one of the Icelandic *Rímur*, as well as a Danish ballad and part of the Shetland *Hildina*.

In accordance with general custom in works of this kind I have discarded the use of accents, unfamiliar symbols, etc., except in a few Norse words which can hardly be anglicised.

My thanks are due to the Syndics of the Cambridge University Press for undertaking the publication of this book, and to the staff for their unfailing courtesy.

To Professor Thuren of Christiania I am indebted for kindly allowing me to print the melodies from his son's *Folkesangen paa Færøerne*. I have also to thank many friends in St Andrews and Cambridge for help which they have kindly given to me in various ways, including Professor Lawson, Dr Maitland Anderson and the staffs of the two University Libraries, and Mr B. Dickins. Especially I wish to thank Professor Chadwick to whom I am indebted for constant help and advice throughout the book.

N. K.

2 November, 1920.

Table of Contents

PART I

SAGAS

PART II

BALLADS

TO

MY SISTER

PART I

SAGAS

THE SAGAS

GENERAL INTRODUCTION

The following stories are taken from the *Fornaldar-sögur Northrlanda*, or 'Stories of Ancient Times relating to the countries of the North'—a collection of Sagas edited by Rafn in 1829–30 and re-edited by Valdimar Ásmundarson in 1886–1891. The stories contained in this collection deal almost exclusively with times anterior to Harold the Fairhaired (c. 860–930) and the colonisation of Iceland, and stop therefore where the better known stories relating to Iceland and the historical kings of Norway begin. Some of them relate to persons and events of the ninth century, while others are concerned with times as remote as the fourth or fifth centuries. Their historical value is naturally far inferior to that of the *Íslendinga Sögur*, or 'Stories of Icelanders' and the *Konunga Sögur*, or 'Stories of the Kings.'

From the literary point of view also the 'Stories of Ancient Times' are generally much inferior to the others. The 'Stories of Icelanders' are derived from oral tradition, which generally goes back in more or less fixed form to the time at which the characters in the stories lived, and they give us a vivid picture of the persons themselves and of the conditions of life in their time. In the 'Stories of Ancient Times,' on the other hand, though there is some element derived from tradition, often apparently of a local character, it is generally very meagre. More often perhaps the source of the stories is to be found in poems, notable instances of which will be found in *Hervarar Saga* and in *Völsunga Saga*. In many cases, however, the stories without doubt contain a large proportion of purely fictitious matter.

The texts of the 'Stories of Ancient Times' which have come down to us date as a rule from the thirteenth and the beginning of the fourteenth centuries, though the actual MSS. themselves are generally later. Most of the stories, however, were probably in existence before this time. The Danish historian Saxo Grammaticus (c. 1200) was familiar with many of them, including the story of Hethin and Högni[1] and one of the scenes recorded in *Hervarar Saga*[2]. And we are told that a story which seems to have corresponded, in its main outlines at least, to the story of Hromund Greipsson was composed and recited at a wedding in Iceland in 1119[3]. But in many cases the materials of our stories were far earlier than this, though they no doubt underwent considerable changes before they assumed their present form.

Indeed many stages in the literary history of the North are represented in the following translations. Of these probably the oldest is that section of the *Hervarar Saga* which deals with the battle between

---

[1] Cf. Saxo Grammaticus, *Dan. Hist.*, Book v, p. 160 (Elton's translation, pp. 197, 198).

[2] Cf. Saxo, *op. cit.*, Book v, p. 166 (Elton's translation, p. 205).

[3] Cf. Introduction to the *Saga of Hromund Greipsson*, p. 58 below.

the Goths and the Huns "at Dylgia and on Dunheith
and upon all the heights of Jösur." The poetry
here included in the saga dates even in its present
form probably from the Viking Age, perhaps from
the tenth century. But the verses themselves do not
appear to be all of the same date. Some of them show
a certain elaboration and a sense of conscious art,
while others are comparatively bare and primitive
in type and contain very early features[1]; and there
is every probability that such poetry was ultimately
derived from poetry composed at a time when the
Goths were still remembered. This is not surprising
in view of the fact that stories relating to the Goths
were popular in English and German heroic poetry,
as well as in the heroic lays of the North. Indeed we
know from Jordanes[2] and elsewhere that heroic poetry
was common among the Goths themselves and that
they were wont to celebrate the deeds of their
ancestors in verse sung to the accompaniment of
the harp.

This poem is no doubt much older than the saga.
Originally it would seem to have been complete in
itself; but many verses have probably been lost.
Thus there can be little doubt that the prose passages
in chs. xii–xv are often merely a paraphrase of lost
verses, though it must not be assumed that all the
prose in this portion of the saga originated in such
a way[3]. "It is difficult to tell...where the prose of

[1] Cf. Heusler and Ranisch, *Eddica Minora* (Dortmund, 1903),
p. xii.
[2] *De Origine Actibusque Getarum* (transl. C. C. Mierow, Princeton,
1915), cap. 5.
[3] Cf. Heusler and Ranisch, *op. cit.*, p. x ff.

the manuscripts is to be taken as standing in the place of lost narrative verses, and where it fills a gap that was never intended to be filled with verse, but was always left to the reciter to be supplied in his own way[1]." The difficulty, however, is greater in some cases than in others. The following picturesque passage from the opening of ch. 14 of the *Hervarar Saga* is a very probable instance of a paraphrase of lost verses:

It happened one morning at sunrise that as Hervör was standing on the summit of a tower over the gate of the fortress, she looked southwards towards the forest and saw clouds of dust, arising from a great body of horse, by which the sun was hidden for a long time. Next she saw a gleam beneath the dust, as though she were gazing on a mass of gold—fair shields overlaid with gold, gilded helmets and white corslets.

The motif of a chief or his lady standing on the pinnacle of a tower of the fort and looking out over the surrounding country for an approaching army is a very common one in ballads. The motif of the above passage from *Hervarar Saga*, including the armour of the foe and the shining shields, occurs in the opening stanzas of the Danish Ballad *De vare syv og syvsindstyve*[2], which probably dates from the fourteenth century (though it may possibly be later[3]) and which derives its material ultimately from old heroic lays[4].

[1] Ker, *Epic and Romance* (London, 1908, 2nd ed.), p. 112.
[2] S. Grundtvig, *Danmarks Gamle Folkeviser* (Copenhagen, 1853–1890), Bd 1, no. 7.
[3] See General Introduction to Part 11, p. 166 below.
[4] Cf. Axel Olrik, *Danske Folkeviser i Udvalg* (Copenhagen and Christiania, 1913), pp. 81, 82.

To the same period approximately as the poem on the battle with the Huns belong the two pieces from the *Older Edda* contained in the *Tháttr*[1] of *Nornagest*. The *Reginsmál* indeed, of which only about half is quoted, may be even earlier than the former (in the form in which it appears in *Hervarar Saga*), while the *Hellride of Brynhild* can hardly be later than the early part of the eleventh century.

A second stage in the literary history of the North is represented by the 'episodic' poems *Hjalmar's Death Song* and the *Waking of Angantyr*, both of which are attributed to the twelfth century by Heusler and Ranisch[2]. Unlike the poem on the battle between the Goths and the Huns, neither of these forms a story complete in itself. They presuppose the existence of a saga in some form or other, presumably oral, dealing at least with the fight at Samsø; and the existence of such a saga in the twelfth century is confirmed by the account of the same event given by Saxo[3].

A third stage in the literary development of the heroic legends is represented by the written saga itself, which has evidently been formed by the welding together, with more or less skill as the case may be, of several distinct stories, and of more than one literary form. A particularly striking instance of this is to be found in the *Hervarar Saga* with its stories of the Heroic and Viking Ages, the poems

---

[1] A. *Tháttr* (pl. *Thættir*) is a story within a story—an episode complete in itself but contained in a long saga.

[2] *Eddica Minora*, pp. xxi, xlii.

[3] *Op. cit.*, Book v, p. 166 (Elton's translation, pp. 204, 205).

dealing with the fight on Samsø, the primitive Riddles of Gestumblindi and the early poem of the battle between the Goths and Huns[1]. Something of the same kind has also taken place in the composition of the *Thættir of Nornagest* and of *Sörli* respectively, though into the former has entered a considerable element of folk-tale which is introduced with a certain *naïveté* and no little skill alongside the old heroic legends. As has been already mentioned, these three sagas, like others of the same type, appear to have been written down in the late thirteenth or the early years of the fourteenth century. On the other hand most if not the whole of the *Saga of Hromund Greipsson* appears to have been composed early in the twelfth century, but we do not know when it was first written down.

A fourth stage is represented by the Icelandic *Rímur* which are for the most part rhyming metrical versions of the sagas and which date from the fourteenth and fifteenth centuries. As an illustration of this stage I have translated a few stanzas from the *Gríplur*, a *Ríma* based on an early form of the story of Hromund Greipsson[2]. The *Rímur* are, so far as we can judge, somewhat wearisome paraphrases of the prose stories, and while the metre and diction are elaborate in the extreme, the treatment of the story is often mechanical and puerile. Comparatively few of the *Rímur* have as yet been published, and the *Gríplur* is the only one known to me which is primarily concerned with any of the sagas contained in this volume.

---

[1] See Introduction to the *Hervarar Saga*, pp. 81–4 below.
[2] See Introduction to the *Gríplur*, p. 171 ff. below.

The ballads, both Faroese and Danish[1], belong to a fifth stage in the life of heroic legend in the North; but their origin and history is by no means so clear as that of the *Rímur*, and it is at present impossible to assign even approximate dates to more than a few of them with any degree of certainty. I have touched on this question at somewhat greater length below[2]; and I would only add here that some Danish and Swedish ballads, e.g. *Ung Sveidal*[3], *Thord af Haffsgaard*[4], and perhaps *Her Aage*[5], appear to be derived more or less directly from poems of the Viking Age, such as *Fjölsvinsmál*, *Thrymskvitha* and *Helgakvitha Hundingsbana I*—without any intermediate prose stage.

A careful study of the Faroese ballads as a whole might enable one to determine something more of the relation of ballads to 'Literature'[6] and of the various ballad forms to one another, such as that of the short and simple *Ballad of Hjalmar and Angantyr* to the longer and more complicated *Ballad of Arngrims Sons*. Simplification and confusion are among the chief characteristics of popular poetry[7]; but it is

[1] Cf. p. 165 ff. below.

[2] Cf. General Introduction to Part II, p. 166 below.

[3] Bugge's edition of the *Saemundar Edda*, p. 352 ff.; also Ker, *Epic and Romance*, p. 114 etc.; Vigfússon and Powell, *Corpus Poeticum Boreale* (Oxford, 1883), Vol. I, p. 501 ff.

[4] *C. P. B.*, Vol. I, pp. 175 and 501 ff.

[5] *C. P. B.*, Vol. I, p. 502 ff.

[6] Always, however, with the proviso that, owing to the avowed literary origin of many of them, the Faroese ballads to some extent form a class by themselves; cf. General Introduction to Part II, p. 166 below.

[7] Cf. Chadwick, *The Heroic Age* (Cambridge, 1912), p. 95.

to be noted that in the case of the *Hervarar Saga*
confusion set in long before the days of the ballad—
as early as the saga itself, where there must surely be
at least one case of repetition of character[1]. In reality,
considering through how many stages the ballad
material has passed, one is amazed at the vitality of
the stories and the amount of original groundwork
preserved. A careful comparison of the *Völsunga Saga*
and the Faroese cycle of ballads generally classed
together as *Sjúrðar Kvæði*—which, be it observed,
were never written down at all till the nineteenth
century—brings out to a degree literally amazing the
conservatism of the ballads on the old heroic themes.

Readers who desire to make further acquaintance
with the 'Stories of Ancient Times' as a whole will
find a further account of the subject in Professor
Craigie's *Icelandic Sagas* (p. 92 ff.). More detailed
accounts will be found in Finnur Jónsson's *Oldnorske og Oldislandske Litteraturs Historie*[2], Vol. II,
pp. 789–847, and in Mogk's *Geschichte der Altnordischen Literatur* in Paul's *Grundriss der Ger-
manischen Philologie*, Ed. II, 1904, Vol. II, pp. 830–
857, while a discussion of the heroic stories will be
found in Professor Chadwick's *Heroic Age*, chs. I–VIII.
For a full bibliography of the texts, translations,
and general literature dealing with the *Fornaldarsögur* collectively, see the annual *Islandica*, Vol. V,
pp. 1–9, compiled by Halldór Hermannsson and
issued by the Cornell University Library, 1912.

[1] Cf. the Introduction to the *Saga of Hervör and Heithrek*,
p. 81 f. below.
[2] Copenhagen, 1901.

INTRODUCTION TO THE THÁTTR
OF NORNAGEST

This story occurs as an episode in the long *Saga of Olaf Tryggvason*—to be distinguished from the shorter *Saga of Olaf Tryggvason* contained in the *Heimskringla* and translated by Morris and Magnússon in the *Saga Library*[1]. The best known manuscript (*F*) of the longer saga is the *Flateyjarbók* which comes from the island of Flatey in Breithifjörth off the west of Iceland, and was written between 1386 and 1394. The second (*S*) is the Codex *Arn. Magn.* 62 in the Royal Library (at Copenhagen), which, like the former, contains a fragment only of the *Saga of Olaf Tryggvason*, but includes the *Tháttr of Nornagest*. This ms. dates, in all probability, from shortly after the middle of the fourteenth century. Finally, besides several paper mss. (comparatively late and unimportant), there is a ms. *A* (number 2845 of the Royal Library at Copenhagen) dating from the fifteenth century, in which the *tháttr* stands by itself.

Rafn[2], in his edition of the *Fornaldarsögur*, based his text of the *tháttr* on *A*; but subsequent examination has rendered it probable that this ms. is hardly independent of *F* which gives an earlier and better

[1] An abridged translation of the longer saga by J. Sephton is published in the *Northern Library*, Vol. II (London, 1898).

[2] *Fornaldarsögur Northrlanda* (Copenhagen, 1829), Introduction, pp. xix, xx.

text. As regards MSS. *F* and *S*, the latter frequently gives a better reading than the former[1]. For this reason it was followed by Bugge[2] who believed it to be the better source. Wilken[3] however held that *F* represents the 'Vulgate' of the *tháttr*, while *S* gives a corrected and edited version. In his edition, therefore, he chiefly followed *F*, though he made use of *S* throughout, and also (for the poems) the *Codex Regius* of the Older Edda. His example has been followed by later editors, including Valdimar Ásmundarson[4], from whose version the following translation has been made. The differences between all three MSS. appear to be very slight, but Ásmundarson's edition approximates more closely to Wilken's than to Rafn's. Indeed the variations between the texts of Wilken's second edition[5] and Ásmundarson are negligible. For a full bibliography of texts, translations, and literature relating to this saga the reader is referred to *Islandica*, Vol. v, p. 32.

The saga itself dates from about 1300[6]. It is derived from tradition, mainly Icelandic; but the various stories contained in it differ greatly from

[1] Wilken, *Die Prosaische Edda nebst Völsungasaga und Nornagests-tháttr* (Paderborn, 1877), p. lxxxv ff.

[2] *Norröne Skrifter af Sagnhistorisk Indhold* (Christiania, 1873).

[3] *Op. cit.*, p. lxxxviii.

[4] See *Fornaldarsögur Northrlanda* (Reykjavík, 1891), Vol. i, pp. 247–266.

[5] The second edition follows the *Codex Regius* in the text of the poems included in the *Tháttr* more closely than did the first edition.

[6] Cf. Finnur Jónsson, *Den Oldnorske og Oldislandske Litteraturs Historie*, Vol. ii, p. 847; also Mogk, *Norwegisch-Isländischen Literatur* (Strassburg, 1904), p. 822.

one another in their historical value. This episode
is probably to be regarded as legendary in part;
and it would seem also to contain a good deal of
conscious fiction.

The *tháttr* falls naturally into three parts. The
framework of the story—the arrival of Guest at the
hall of Olaf Tryggvason, his inclusion in the King's
retinue, and his baptism—forms a whole in itself
and contains nothing inherently improbable save
the manner of his death, where the folk-tale element
creeps in. The first 'story within a story,' the
account that Guest gives of his wanderings and more
especially of the adventures of Sigurth, is legendary
—or perhaps rather made up from old legends with
the help of the *Edda* poems. As in the case of the
Anglo-Saxon poem *Widsith*—and indeed to a much
greater extent—the persons who figure in the
stranger's stories lived in reality in widely different
ages. Sigurth and his brothers-in-law belong to the
early part of the fifth century, Harold the Fairhaired
and the sons of Lothbrok to the latter part of the
ninth century. Other characters such as Guthmund
of Glasisvellir who is mentioned in the first chapters
are probably mythical.

The third part, which is perhaps the most interesting part of the *tháttr*, is the passage in which
Guest explains how he came by his name. There
can be no doubt that here we are in the region of
pure folk-tale. The story of the visit of the Norns
shows a very remarkable resemblance to the Greek
legend of Althaea and Meleager. The same motif
appears to some extent in the mediaeval French
romances of *Ogier the Dane*, and is familiar to every-

one in a slightly different form as the first part of
the German folk-tale, *Sleeping Beauty*, where the
reference to spinning should be noted.

The poetry contained in this *tháttr*, unlike that in
the *Hervarar Saga*, is all taken from the *Older Edda*.
One of the poems, the *Hellride of Brynhild*, is given
almost complete and there are long extracts from
Reginsmál. There are, however, some references to
poems which no longer exist[1].

In many respects the story of Nornagest is among
the most interesting of the Romantic Sagas. It gives
a vivid picture of life in a northern court—the
naïveté and friendliness of the conversation; the
personal interest that the King took in his men; the
intimacy and directness and simplicity of the intercourse between them. There is something, too, of the
same boyish indulgence—e.g. in King Olaf's attitude
towards the wager—which one notices in Hrolf
Kraki's talk with Vögg[2]. Yet combined with the
amiability of both kings is a certain natural dignity
which is very convincing.

THE THÁTTR OF NORNAGEST

I. The story goes that on one occasion when
King Olaf Tryggvason was living at Trondhjem, it
chanced that a man came to him late in the day and
addressed him respectfully. The King welcomed him
and asked him who he was, and he said that his name
was Guest.

[1] Cf. p. 19 below and note (p. 222).
[2] Cf. *Skáldskaparmál*, ch. 3; also *Hrólfs Saga Kraka*, ch. 42.

The King answered: "You shall be guest here, whatever you are called."

Guest said: "I have told you my name truly, Sire, and I will gladly receive your hospitality if I may."

The King told him he could have it readily. But since the day was far spent, the King would not enter into conversation with his guest; for he was going soon to vespers, and after that to dinner, and then to bed and to sleep.

Now on that same night King Olaf Tryggvason was lying awake in his bed and saying his prayers, while all the other men in the hall were asleep. Then the King noticed that an elf or spirit of some kind had come into the hall, though all the doors were locked. He made his way past the beds of the men who were asleep there, one after another, and at last reached the bed of a man at the far end.

Then the elf stopped and said: "An empty house, and a mighty strong bolt on the door! People say that the King is the wisest of men. If he were as clever in things of this kind as they say he would not sleep so soundly."

After that he vanished through the door, locked as it was.

Early next morning the King sent his servant to find out who had occupied that bed over night, and it proved to have been the stranger. The King ordered him to be summoned before him and asked him whose son he was.

He answered: "My father's name was Thorth. He was a Dane and was called 'The Contentious,' and lived at a place called Groening in Denmark."

"You are a well set-up man," said the King.

Guest was bold of speech, and bigger in build than most men. He looked strong but was somewhat advanced in years. He asked the King if he might stay for a while in his retinue. The King asked if he were baptised. Guest said that he had been prime-signed but not baptised. The King said that he was free to remain in his retinue, but added:

"You will not remain long unbaptised with me."

The reason for the elf's remark about the bolt was that Guest had crossed himself, that evening like other men, but was in reality still a heathen.

The King said: "Can you do anything in the way of sport or music?"

He replied that he could play the harp and tell stories which people enjoyed.

Then said the King: "King Svein has no right to let unbaptised men leave his kingdom and wander about from one country to another."

Guest replied: "You must not blame the King of the Danes for this, for it is a long time since I left Denmark. In fact it was a long time before the Emperor Otto burnt the Dane-work and forced King Harold Gormsson and Earl Haakon the Heathen to become Christians."

The King questioned Guest about many subjects and he always gave him good and intelligent answers. Men say that it was in the third year of King Olaf's reign that Guest came to him.

In this year also there came to him two men called Grim who were sent by Guthmund from Glasisvellir. They brought to the King as a present from Guthmund two horns which were also called 'Grim.'

They had also some further business with the King to which we will return later.

As for Guest, he remained with the King, and had a place at the far end of the visitors' seats. He was a man of breeding and had good manners, and was popular and much respected by everyone.

II. A little before Yule, Ulf the Red and his following came home. He had been engaged on the King's business all summer, for he had been appointed to guard the coasts of 'The Bay' against Danish raids. He never failed to be with King Olaf at mid-winter.

Ulf had many fine treasures to bring to the King, which he had got during the summer, and one gold ring in particular which was called Hnituth. It was welded together in seven places and each piece had a different colour. It was made of much finer gold than rings usually are. The ring had been given to Ulf by a landowner called Lothmund, and before that it had belonged to King Half, from whom the Halfsrekkar take their name. The ring had come to them as forced tribute from King Halfdan Ylfing. Lothmund had asked Ulf in return for it that he would guard his home with the support of King Olaf, and Ulf had promised to do so.

Now King Olaf was keeping Yule in magnificent style at his court in Trondhjem; and it was on the eighth day of Yule that Ulf gave him the gold ring Hnituth. The King thanked him for the gift as well as for all the faithful service which he had constantly rendered him.

The ring was passed round the building in which the drinking was going on.—As yet no halls had been built in Norway. Now each man showed it to his neighbour and they thought that they had never seen such fine gold as that of which the ring was made. At last it came to the guest-table, and so to the guest who had just arrived. He looked at the ring and handed it back on the palm of his hand—the hand in which he had been holding his drinking horn. He was not much impressed with the treasure, and made no remarks about it, but went on jesting with his companions. A serving-man was pouring out drink at the end of the guest-table.

"Do you not like the ring?" he asked.

They said: "We all like it very much except the new-comer. He can't see anything in it; but we think he can't appreciate it simply because he doesn't care for things of this kind."

The serving-man went up the hall to the King and told him exactly what the guests had said, adding that the new-comer had taken little note of the treasure, valuable as it was, when it was shown to him.

Then the King remarked: "The new-comer probably knows more than you think: he must come to me in the morning and tell me a story."

Now he and the other guests at the farthest table were talking among themselves. They asked the new-comer where he had seen a better ring or even one as good as this.

"Since you evidently think it strange," said he, "that I make so little of it, I may say that I have certainly seen gold which is in no way inferior, but actually better."

The King's men now laughed heartily and said that that promised good sport, adding:

"Will you agree to wager with us that you have seen gold as good as this, and prove it? We will stake four marks in current coin against your knife and belt; and the King shall decide who is in the right."

Then said Guest: "I will neither be made a laughing-stock for you nor fail to keep the wager which you offer. And I will certainly lay a wager with you on the spot, and stake exactly what you have suggested, and the King shall judge who is in the right."

Then they stopped talking, and Guest took his harp and played it well till far into the evening, so that it was a joy to all who heard him. What he rendered best was *The Harping of Gunnar*; and last of all he played the ancient *Wiles of Guthrun*, neither of which they had heard before. And after that they went to sleep for the night.

III. In the morning the King rose early and heard Mass; and after that he went to breakfast with his retinue. And when he had taken his place in the high seat, the guests came up to him, and Guest with them; and they told him all about their agreement and the wager which they had made.

"I am not much taken with your wager," replied the King, "although it is your own money that you are staking. I suspect that the drink must have gone to your heads; and I think you would do well to give it up, especially if Guest agrees."

"My wish is," replied Guest, "that the whole agreement should stand."

"It looks to me, Guest," said the King, "as if it was my men rather than you whose tongues have got them into trouble; but we will soon put it to the test."

After that they left him and went to drink; and when the drinking tables were removed, the King summoned Guest and spoke to him as follows:

"Now is the time for you to produce the gold if you have any, so that I can decide your wager."

"As you will, Sire!" replied Guest.

Then he felt in a pouch which he had with him, and took out of it a fob which he untied, and then handed something to the King.

The King saw that it was a piece of a saddle-buckle and that it was of exceedingly fine gold. Then he bade them bring the ring Hnituth; and when they did so, the King compared the ring and the piece of gold and said:

"I have no doubt whatever that the gold which Guest has shown us is the finer, and anyone who looks at it must think so too."

Everybody agreed with the King. Then he decided the wager in Guest's favour, and the other guests came to the conclusion that they had made fools of themselves over the business.

Then Guest said: "Take your money and keep it yourselves, for I don't need it; but don't make any more wagers with strangers, for you never know when you may hit upon someone who has both seen and heard more than you have.—I thank you, Sire, for your decision!"

Then the King said: "Now I want you to tell me where you got that gold from, which you carry about with you."

Guest replied: "I am loth to tell you, because no-one will believe what I have to say about it."

"Let us hear it all the same," said the King, "for

you promised before that you would tell us your story."

"If I tell you the history of this piece of gold," replied Guest, "I expect you will want to hear the rest of my story along with it."

"I expect that that is just what will happen," said the King.

IV. "Then I will tell you how once I went south into the land of the Franks. I wanted to see for myself what sort of a prince Sigurth the son of Sigmund was, and to discover if the reports which had reached me of his great beauty and courage were true. Nothing happened worth mentioning until I came to the land of the Franks and met King Hjalprek. He had a great court around him. Sigurth, the son of Sigmund, the son of Völsung, and of Hjördis, the daughter of Eylimi, was there at that time. Sigmund had fallen in battle against the sons of Hunding, and Hjördis had married Alf the son of King Hjalprek. There Sigurth grew up together with all the other sons of King Sigmund. Among these were Sinfjötli and Helgi, who surpassed all men in strength and stature. Helgi slew King Hunding, thereby earning the name Hundingsbani. The third son was called Hamund. Sigurth, however, outstripped all his brothers, and it is a well-known fact that he was the noblest of all warrior princes, and the very model of a king in heathen times.

At that time, Regin, the son of Hreithmar, had also come to King Hjalprek. He was a dwarf in stature, but there was no-one more cunning than he. He was a wise man, but malign and skilled in magic. Regin taught Sigurth many things and was devoted to him. He told him about his birth and his wondrous adventures.

And when I had been there a little while, I entered Sigurth's service like many others. He was very popular with everybody, because he was friendly and unassuming, and generous to all.

V. It chanced one day that we came to Regin's house and Sigurth was made welcome there. Then Regin spoke these verses:

> The son of Sigmund cometh to our hall,
> A valiant warrior. It must needs befall
> That I, less doughty and oppressed with age,
> Shall fall a victim to his wolfish rage.

> But I will cherish Yngvi's valorous heir,
> Since Fate hath sent him hither to our care,
> Train him to be, in valour and in worth,
> The mightiest and most famous prince on earth.

At this time, Sigurth was constantly in Regin's company. Regin told him much about Fafnir—how he dwelt upon Gnitaheith in the form of a serpent, and also of his wondrous size. Regin made for Sigurth a sword called Gram. It was so sharp that when he thrust it into the River Rhine it cut in two a flock of wool which he had dropped into the river and which was drifting down stream, cutting it just as clean as it did the water itself. Later on, Sigurth clove Regin's stithy with the sword. After that Regin urged Sigurth to slay his brother Fafnir and Sigurth recited this verse:

> The sons of Hunding would laugh loud and high,
> Who shed the life-blood of King Eylimi,
> If that his grandson bold should more desire
> Rings of red gold than vengeance for his sire.

After that Sigurth made ready an expedition to attack the sons of Hunding; and King Hjalprek gave him many men and some warships. Hamund, Sigurth's brother, was with him on this venture, and so was Regin the dwarf. I was present too, and they called me Nornagest. King Hjalprek had got to know me when he was in Denmark with Sigmund the son of Völsung. At that time, Sigmund was married to Borghild, but they parted because Borghild killed Sinfjötli the son of Sigmund by poison. Then Sigmund went south to the land of the Franks and married Hjördis, the daughter of King Eylimi. The sons of Hunding slew him, so Sigurth had both his father and grandfather to avenge.

Helgi, the son of Sigmund, who was called Hundingsbani, was the brother of Sigurth who was afterwards called Fafnisbani. Helgi, Sigurth's brother, had slain King Hunding and three of his sons, Eyjulf, Hervarth, and Hjörvarth, but Lyngvi and his two remaining brothers, Alf and Heming, escaped. They were exceedingly famous for exploits and accomplishments of every kind; but Lyngvi surpassed all his brothers. They were very skilled in magic. They had reduced many petty kings to subjection, and slain many champions, and burnt many cities. They had worked the greatest havoc with their raids in Spain and in the land of the Franks. But at that time the Imperial Power had not yet been transferred to the regions north of the Alps. The sons of Hunding had seized the realm which had belonged to Sigurth in the land of the Franks, and they had very large forces there.

VI. Now I must tell you how Sigurth prepared
for battle against the sons of Hunding. He had got
together a large and well-armed host, and Regin was
a mighty man in the councils of the force. He had
a sword which was called Rithil and which he had
forged himself. Sigurth asked Regin to lend him
the sword. He did so, begging him to slay Fafnir
when he should return from this adventure, and this
Sigurth promised to do.

After that we sailed away south along the coast,
and then we met with a great storm raised by witch-
craft, and many believed that it had been stirred up
by the sons of Hunding. After this we hugged the
shore somewhat more closely, and then we saw a
man on a rocky promontory which jutted out from
the cliffs. He wore a green cloak and dark breeches,
and had high laced boots on his feet, and carried a
spear in his hand. This man addressed us in the
following stanza:

> What folk are ye who ride the sea-king's steed,
> Mounting the lofty billows, and proceed
> Athwart the tossing main? Drenched is your sail,
> Nor can your ships against the wind prevail.

Regin replied:

> Hither come we with Sigurth o'er the foam,
> Whom ocean breezes blow to our last home.—
> Full soon the breakers, higher than the prow
> Will sink our 'ocean-steeds'; but who art thou?

The man in the cloak replied:

> Hnikar the name men did for me employ,
> Young Völsung, when I gave the raven joy
> Of carnage. Call me either of the two—
> Fjölnir or Feng, but let me fare with you.

Then we steered towards the land and the wind
fell immediately; and Sigurth bade the man come
on board. He did so, and a fair breeze sprang up.
The man sat down at Sigurth's feet and was very
friendly, asking if Sigurth would like to hear some
advice from him. Sigurth said that he would, and
added that he had an idea that Hnikar could give
people very helpful advice if he were willing to turn
it to their advantage. Then Sigurth said to the man
in the cloak:

O Hnikar, since you know the destiny
Of gods and men, declare this unto me.—
Which are the omens that should most delight
When swords are swinging and a man must fight?

Hnikar replied:

Many propitious signs, if men could know,
Appear when swords are swinging to and fro.
I hold a warrior has a trusty guide
When a dark raven hovers at his side.

I hold it too for a propitious sign
If men to make a journey should design,
And, coming out of doors, see close at hand
Two gallant warriors in the pathway stand.

And if you hear beneath the rowan tree
A howling wolf, the sound spells luck to thee,
And luck shall helmed warriors bring to thee,
If thou such warriors art the first to see.

Facing the sinking and late shining light
Of the Moon's sister, warriors should not fight.
Victory is theirs who, eager for the fray,
Can clearly see to order their array.

I hold it no occasion for delight
When a man stumbles as he goes to fight;
For guileful spirits dog him on his way
With mischief-bearing looks throughout the fray

A man of wisdom, as each day goes past,
Washes, and combs his hair, and breaks his fast.
He knows not where by evening he may be.—
Stumbling is bad luck, boding ill to thee.

And after that we sailed southwards along the
coast of Holstein and to the east of Friesland, and
there we landed. The sons of Hunding heard at once
of our expedition and gathered an army; and they
soon had a larger force than we had, and when we
encountered them there was a great battle. Lyngvi
was the most valiant of the brothers in every onset,
though they all fought bravely. Sigurth's attack was
so fierce that everyone shrank before him, when they
saw that they were threatened by the sword Gram.
There was no need to reproach Sigurth with lack of
courage. And when he and Lyngvi met, they exchanged many blows and fought with the greatest
valour. Then there was a lull in the battle, for people
turned to watch the single combat. For a long time
neither of them was able to inflict a wound on the
other, so skilled in arms were they.

Then Lyngvi's brothers made a fierce attack and
slew many of our men, while others took to flight. Then
Hamund, Sigurth's brother, rushed to meet them, and
I joined him, and then there was another encounter.

The end of the affair between Sigurth and Lyngvi
was that Sigurth made him prisoner and had him
fettered. And when Sigurth joined us, matters very
soon changed. Then the sons of Hunding fell and
all their host; but then night was coming on. And
when day dawned, Hnikar had vanished, and he was
never seen again. We came to the conclusion that it
must in reality have been Othin.

A discussion then took place as to what death Lyngvi should suffer; Regin counselled that the 'blood eagle' should be carved on his back. Then I handed to Regin his sword and with it he carved Lyngvi's back till he had severed the ribs from the spine; and then he drew out the lungs. Thus died Lyngvi with great courage.

Then Regin said:

> Full seldom has a bolder warrior
> Reddened the earth than Sigmund's murderer.
> Hugin he feasted. Now with biting sword
> The 'bloody eagle' on his back is scored.

Great spoil was taken there. Sigurth's sailors got the whole of it because he would not take any himself. The clothes and weapons taken were worth much gold.

Afterwards Sigurth slew Fafnir, and Regin also, because Regin had intended to deal treacherously with him. Sigurth took Fafnir's gold and rode away with it, and from that time on he was called Fafnisbani.

After that he rode up to Hindarheith where he found Brynhild. What passed between them is told in the story of Sigurth Fafnisbani.

VII. Later on Sigurth married Guthrun the daughter of King Gjuki and then stayed for a while with his brothers-in-law, the sons of Gjuki. I returned to the North with Sigurth and was with him in Denmark, and I was also with him when Sigurth Hring sent his brothers-in-law, the sons of Gandalf, to Gunnar and Högni, the sons of Gjuki, and demanded that they should pay him tribute, threatening them with invasion in case they refused. But they

decided to defend their country. Thereupon Gandalf's
sons challenged the sons of Gjuki to a pitched battle
on the frontier, and then returned home; but the
sons of Gjuki asked Sigurth Fafnisbani to go to
battle with them, and he agreed to do so. I was still
with Sigurth at that time. Then we sailed again
northwards along the coast of Holstein and landed
at a place called Jarnamotha. Not far from the
landing place hazel-wood poles had been set up to
mark where the fight was to take place.

Then we saw many ships sailing from the north
under the command of the sons of Gandalf. Then the
two hosts charged one another fiercely. Sigurth
Hring was not there, because he had to defend his
own land, Sweden, against the inroads of the Kurir
and Kvænir. Sigurth was a very old man at that
time. Then the forces came into collision, and there
was a great battle and much slaughter. The sons of
Gandalf fought bravely, for they were exceptionally
big and strong.

In that host there appeared a big strong man who
made such slaughter of men and horses that no-one
could withstand him, for he was more like a giant
than a man. Gunnar bade Sigurth go and attack
the scoundrel, adding that as things were, there
would be no success. So Sigurth made ready to
encounter the mighty man, and some others went
with him, but most of them were far from eager.

We quickly came upon the mighty man, and
Sigurth asked him his name and whence he came.
He said that he was Starkath, the son of Storverk,
and that he came from the North, from Fenhring
in Norway. Sigurth said that he had heard reports

of him and generally little to his credit, adding that no mercy ought to be shown towards such people.

Starkath said: "Who is this man who casts insults in my teeth?"

Sigurth told him who he was.

Starkath said: "Are you called Fafnisbani?"

Sigurth said he was.

Then Starkath sought to escape, but Sigurth pursued him and swung aloft the sword Gram and struck him on the jaw with the hilt so hard that two molars fell out of his mouth; it was a stunning blow.

Then Sigurth bade the cur take himself off, and Starkath went away, and I picked up one of the teeth and carried it off with me. It is now used on a bell-rope at Lund in Denmark and weighs seven ounces; and people go and look at it there as a curiosity.

As soon as Starkath had run away, the sons of Gandalf took to flight, and we captured great booty; and after that Sigurth went home to his realm and remained there for a while.

VIII. A short time after, we heard that Starkath had committed a foul murder, slaying King Ali in his bath.

It chanced one day that as Sigurth Fafnisbani was riding to some gathering or other, he rode into a muddy pool, and his horse Grani leapt up so wildly that his saddle-girth burst asunder and the buckle fell to the ground. And when I saw where it lay shining in the mud, I picked it up and handed it to Sigurth; but he said that I might keep it. It was that very piece of gold that you were looking at a short time ago. Then Sigurth got down from his horse, and I rubbed it down and washed the mud off it; and I pulled a lock of hair out of its tail as a proof of its great size.

Then Guest showed the lock and it was seven ells long.

King Olaf said: "I think your stories are very entertaining."

Everybody praised his stories and his talent.

Then the King wanted him to tell them much more about the adventures he had met with on his travels. So Guest told them many amusing stories till late in the evening. It was then time to go to bed; but next morning the King sent for Guest, and wanted to talk to him still further.

The King said: "I can't quite make out your age and how you can be old enough to have been present when these events took place. You will have to tell another story so as to make us better acquainted with things of this kind."

Guest replied: "I suspected before that you would want to hear another of my stories, if I told you what had happened about the gold."

"You must certainly tell me some more," replied the King.

IX. "I must tell you then," Guest began, "that I went north to Denmark and there settled down on my estate, for my father had died a short time before; and a little later I heard of the death of Sigurth and the sons of Gjuki, and I felt that that was news indeed."

"What was the cause of Sigurth's death?" asked the King.

Guest replied: "It is generally believed that Guthorm the son of Gjuki ran a sword through him while he was asleep in bed with Guthrun. On the other hand, Germans say that Sigurth was slain out in the forest. In the *Guthrúnar-rætha* again it is stated that Sigurth and the sons of Gjuki had ridden to a gathering and that they slew him then. But one thing is agreed by all—that they set on him when he was down and off his guard, and that they were guilty of gross treachery towards him."

Then one of the retinue asked:

"How did Brynhild behave then?"

Guest answered: "Brynhild then slew seven of her slaves and five handmaidens, and ran herself through with a sword, commanding that she should be taken to the pyre along with these people and burned beside Sigurth. This was done, one pile being made for Sigurth and another for Brynhild, and he was burned first, and then Brynhild. She was taken in a chariot with a canopy of velvet and silk which was all ablaze with gold, and thus was she burnt."

Then Guest was asked if Brynhild had chanted a lay after she was dead. He replied that she had, and they asked him to recite it if he could.

Then Guest said: "As Brynhild was being driven to the pyre on the way to Hell, she was brought near some cliffs where an ogress dwelt. The ogress was standing outside the doors of her cave and wore a skin kirtle and was of a blackish hue. She carried a long faggot in her hand and cried:

'This will I contribute to your burning, Brynhild. It would have been better if you had been burned while you were still alive, before you were guilty of getting such a splendid man as Sigurth Fafnisbani slain. I was always friendly to him and therefore I shall attack

you in a reproachful song which will make you hated
by everybody who hears what you have done.'

After that Brynhild and the ogress chanted to
one another.

The ogress sang as follows:

Thou shalt not be suffered to pass through my courts
 With their pillars of stone in my mansion drear,—
Better far wert thou busied at home with thy needle!
 Not thine is the husband thou followest here.

Inconstant soul, why comest thou hither?
 From the land of the Romans why visit'st thou me?
Full many a wolf hast thou made be partaker
 Of the life-blood of men who were butchered by thee!

 Then cried Brynhild:

Upbraid me no more from thy rock bound dwelling
 For battles I fought in the days of old.—
Thou wilt not be deemed to be nobler of nature
 Than I, wheresoever our story is told!

 The Ogress:

In an evil hour, O Buthli's daughter,
 In an evil hour wert thou brought to birth.—
The Sons of Gjuki thou gavest to slaughter,
 Their noble dwellings thou rased'st to earth.

 Brynhild:

A true account, if thou carest to hearken,
 O thou lying soul, will I tell to thee;—
How empty of love and o'ershadowed by falsehood
 The life that the Gjukings had destined for me!

Atli's daughter was I, yet the monarch bold-hearted
 Assigned me a home neath the shade of the oak.
But twelve summers old, if thou carest to hearken,
 Was this maid when her vows to the hero she spoke.

Hjalmgunnar the Old, of the Gothic nation,
  Great chief, on the pathway to Hell did I speed;
And victory granted to Auth's young brother;
  Then Othin's dread fury was roused at my deed.

Then a phalanx of bucklers did Othin set round me
  On Skatalund's heights, shields crimson and white,—
Bade only that prince break the slumber that bound me
  Who knew naught of terror, nor shrank from the fight.

And flames high towering and fiercely raging
  Round my Southern hall did he set in a ring:
None other was destined to pass through in safety
  Save the hero who treasure of Fafnir should bring.

The generous hero with treasure a-gleaming,
  The Danish viking on Grani rode,—
Foremost champion in deeds of valour—
  Where my foster-father had his abode.

As brother with sister we slept together;
  Eight nights' space he lay at my side.
There were we happy and slumbered idly,
  Nor loving caresses did ever betide.

Yet Guthrun the daughter of Gjuki reviled me,
  That I in the arms of her lover had slept.
O then was I 'ware of the thing I desired not—
  The truth of my marriage from me had they kept.

All too long against storms of adversity struggling
  Both women and men seek their fortunes to right;
But I with my Sigurth shall end my life's battle
  At last. Now depart from me, daughter of Night!

Then the ogress gave a horrible shriek and leapt into the cliff."

Then the King's followers cried: "That's fine! Go on and tell us some more!"

But the King said: "You need not tell us any

more about things of that kind." Then he continued: "Were you ever with the sons of Lothbrok?"

Guest replied: "I was only with them for a short time; I joined them when they were making an expedition to the south in the neighbourhood of the Alps, and when they destroyed Vifilsborg. Panic spread everywhere at their approach, for they were victorious wherever they went. They were intending at the time to go to Rome. It chanced one day that a certain man came up to King Björn Ironside and saluted him. The King received him in a friendly way and asked him whence he came. He said that he had come from the south, from Rome.

The King asked him: 'How long is the journey there?'

He replied: 'You can see here, O King, the shoes which I am wearing.'

Then he took iron-bound shoes from his feet, and the tops of them were very thick, but underneath they were all torn.

'You can see now how severely my shoes have suffered,' said he, 'and tell by that what a long way it is from here to Rome.'

'It must be a very long way,' said the King; 'I shall turn back and give up the idea of attacking the territories of Rome.'

And the result was that they went no further on their way; and everyone thought it extraordinary that they should change their minds so suddenly at the word of one man, when they had all their plans laid. So after this the sons of Lothbrok went back to their homes in the north, and made no further raids in the south."

The King said: "It is clear that the saints in Rome would not allow them to make their way there. The man you spoke of must have been a Spirit sent from God to make them change their minds so quickly, so as not to bring destruction on Rome, the most holy place of Jesus Christ."

X. Then the King asked Guest: "Amongst the kings whom you have visited, whose was the court that you liked best?"

Guest replied: "I enjoyed most being with Sigurth and the sons of Gjuki; but the sons of Lothbrok were those who allowed most freedom to their followers to live as they liked. Then again the richest place was that of Eric at Upsala; but King Harold the Fairhaired was more exacting than any of the kings I have mentioned in the duties that he imposed on his followers. I was with King Hlöthver too in the land of the Saxons, and there I was prime-signed; for it was not possible to remain with him otherwise, because the Christian religion was carefully observed there. That was the place I liked best on the whole."

The King said: "You can give us a great deal of information whatever question we ask you."

The King then asked Guest many further questions, and Guest told him everything clearly, and finally he said:

"Now I must tell you why I am called Norna-gest."

The King said he would like to hear.

XI. Guest began: "I was brought up at my father's home at a place called Groening. My father was a wealthy man and kept house in great style. At that time wise women used to go about the country. They were called 'spae-wives,' and they

3—2

foretold people's futures. For this reason people used
to invite them to their houses and gave them hospitality and bestowed gifts on them at parting.

My father did the same, and they came to him
with a great following to foretell my fate. I was lying
in my cradle when the time came for them to prophesy
about me, and two candles were burning above
me. Then they foretold that I should be a favourite
of Fortune, and a greater man than any of my kindred
or forbears—greater even than the sons of the chief
men in the land; and they said that all would come
to pass just as it has done. But the youngest Norn
thought that she was not receiving enough attention
compared with the other two, since they were
held in high account yet did not consult her about
these prophecies. There was also a great crowd of
roughs present, who pushed her off her seat, so that
she fell to the ground. She was much vexed at this
and called out loudly and angrily, telling them to
stop prophesying such good things about me:

'For I ordain that the boy shall live no longer than
that candle burns which is alight beside him.'

Then the eldest spae-wife took the candle and
extinguished it and bade my mother take charge of
it and not light it until the last day of my life. After
that the spae-wives went away, and my father gave
them good gifts at parting. When I was full-grown,
my mother gave me the candle to take charge of: I
have it with me now."

The King said: "Why have you come here to me
now?"

Guest replied: "The idea that came into my mind
was this: I expected that I should get good luck from

you, because I have heard you highly praised by good and wise men."

The King said: "Will you receive holy baptism now?"

Guest replied: "Yes, I will, since you advise it."

So it came to pass; and the King took him into his favour and made him one of his retinue. Guest became a very good Christian and loyally followed the King's rules of life. He was also popular with everybody.

XII. It happened one day that the King asked Guest: "How much longer would you live if you could choose?"

Guest replied: "Only a short time, please God!"

The King said: "What will happen if you take your candle now?"

Thereupon Guest took his candle out of the frame of his harp. The King ordered it to be lighted, and this was done. And when the candle was lighted it soon began to burn away.

Then the King said to Guest: "How old are you?"

And Guest replied: "I am now three hundred years old."

"You are an old man," observed the King.

Then Guest laid himself down and asked them to anoint him with oil. The King ordered it to be done, and when it was finished there was very little of the candle left unburnt. Then it became clear that Guest was drawing near to his end, and his spirit passed just as the torch flickered out; and they all marvelled at his passing. The King also set great store by his stories and held that the account which he had given of his life was perfectly true.

INTRODUCTION TO THE THÁTTR
OF SÖRLI

This story, like the last, is taken from the long *Saga of Olaf Tryggvason* contained in the *Flateyjarbók*, Vol. I, pp. 275–283. Its connection, however, with the story of that King is of the slightest. According to the opinion of Finnur Jónsson[1] the story in its present form dates from the first half of the fourteenth century.

This story, like the *Tháttr of Nornagest*, shows evidence of a definite structural plan and falls into three distinct parts. In the first two chapters the scene is laid among the gods, and the story is set in motion by the forging of a necklace for the goddess Freyja by some dwarfs. This is stolen by Loki and given to Othin, who refuses to restore it to Freyja till she promises to bring about a perpetual battle between two mighty kings.

Then in chs. III and IV we have an account of the adventures of a Viking prince named Sörli, from whom the story takes its (somewhat inappropriate) title[2]. Sörli comes into contact (first as an enemy, later as a friend) with another prince called Högni, and this leads up to the main theme—the friendship and subsequent quarrel of Hethin and Högni, in

[1] *Oldnorske og Oldislandske Litteraturs Historie*, Vol. II, p. 837.

[2] The life of this prince is told at length in another saga—*Sörla Saga Sterka* which is published in Vol. III of Ásmundarson's edition of the *Fornaldarsögur*.

whose tragic fate Freyja's promise is fulfilled. The perpetual battle between these two heroes is finally ended by one of Olaf Tryggvason's men, and it is through this that the story comes to be introduced into his Saga.

The story of Hethin and Högni was a favourite one in the North. It is told in *Skáldskaparmál*, ch. 49, and in Saxo Grammaticus' *Danish History*, Book v (Elton, pp. 195–198). The earliest Norse reference to it is to be found in Bragi's *Ragnarsdrápa*, str. 3–7. The story must also have been well known in the Orkneys, since we find the following verses in the *Háttalykill* by Jarl Rögnvald (1136–58) and an Icelandic skald Hall who flourished 1140–48[1].

> Who planned to carry off Hild?
> Who fight all day long?
> Who will be reconciled at last?
> Who incited the kings?
> Hethin planned to carry off Hild;
> The Hjathningar are always fighting;
> They will be reconciled at last;
> Hild incited the host.

> Who reddens the keen blades?
> Who chops meat for the wolf?
> Who makes showers of helmets?
> Who stirred up strife?
> Harold reddened the keen blades;
> The host chops meat for the wolf;
> Högni makes the shower of helmets;
> Hjarrandi stirred up strife!

In the Shetlands the story survived down to modern times in the form of a ballad known as

[1] Cf. Finnur Jónsson, *op. cit.*, Vol. II, pp. 34, 35.

Hildina, which was taken down by George Low[1] from the recitation of an old man on the Isle of Foula in 1774. The Norwegian dialect (Norn) in which it is composed is so obscure as we have it in Low's script as to be almost untranslatable, though a serious attempt at its interpretation has been made by Dr M. Hægstad in *Skrifter udgivne af Viden-skabsselskabet i Christiania*, 1900 (*Historisk-Filosofisk Klasse*, 11), with a very full discussion of all the linguistic difficulties involved[2]. According to Low, "The subject is a strife between a King of Norway and an Earl of Orkney, on account of the hasty marriage of the Earl with the King's daughter in her father's absence." Further on[3] he gives the substance of the ballad at greater length:

An Earl of Orkney, in some of his rambles on the coast of Norway, saw and fell in love with the King's daughter of the country. As their passion happened to be reciprocal he carried her off in her father's absence, who was engaged in war with some of his distant neighbours. On his return, he followed the fugitives to Orkney, accompanied by his army, to revenge on the Earl the rape of his daughter. On his arrival there, Hildina (which was her name) first spied him, and advised her now husband to go and attempt to pacify the King. He did so, and by his appearance and promises brought the King so over as to be satisfied with the match.

After this, with the introduction of a courtier Hiluge the story proceeds in a form totally different from anything found in the *þáttr*, though an attempt

[1] Cf. *A Tour through the Islands of Orkney and Schetland*, by George Low, edited by J. A. Anderson (Kirkwall, 1879), p. 108 ff.

[2] On p. 217 ff. below I have attempted a translation of the first twelve stanzas from Hægstad's corrected text.

[3] *Op. cit.*, p. 113.

has been made to connect it with the second part of the German poem *Kudrun*.

The story of Hethin and Högni however was not confined to Norway and its colonies; indeed it seems to have been popular throughout the whole Teutonic world. It forms the subject of the first part of the mediaeval German poem *Kudrun*, and characters from the story are mentioned in the Anglo-Saxon poems *Widsith*, l. 21, and *Deor*, l. 36 ff.

For a treatment of the different versions of the story as it was known to men of old, the reader may be referred to Miss Clarke's *Sidelights on Teutonic History during the Migration Period* (Cambridge, 1911), p. 190 ff., and to Chambers' *Widsith*, p. 100 ff. It may be mentioned here that in the main points of the story—the carrying off of Hild and the subsequent pursuit by the father—all the versions are agreed. The German version, however, differs in many respects from those of the North (except that of the *Hildina*)—especially in the fact that the combatants become reconciled. The various Scandinavian versions of the story also differ somewhat in detail among themselves. The story translated below is the only one which mentions the slaying by Hethin of Högni's wife, and it is only here that Hethin is described as being of foreign origin. Moreover this is the only version in which the goddess Freyja is made responsible for the Unending Battle. Indeed the supernatural element, and especially the influence of charms and spells, is more prominent in this version than in any of·the others. It is only here, too, that we find the story of Göndul and the "potion of forgetfulness." On the other hand our version

contains no reference to the statement made in
Skáldskaparmál and Saxo that it was Hild who by
her magic spells restored the dead to life each night.

In our version of the story the character of
Hild is left wholly undeveloped. Indeed the writers
of the Romantic Sagas are always so much more
interested in incident than in character that highly
individualised personality is rare. Even when, as
in the case of Hervör[1], the very nature of the
story presents an interesting and somewhat unusual
personality, we are sometimes left with a feeling of
dissatisfaction and a conviction that the writer did
not realise the full merits and possibilities of his
material. Högni is the usual type of hot-headed
implacable sea-rover. The character of Hethin,
however, presents some interesting features and
strikes us as more modern in conception. Naturally
gentle of disposition, he had been forced by malignant
powers into a situation foreign to his nature. Hardly
characteristic of a viking chief are his genuine regret
for the harm he had done and his anxiety that the men
of Högni and himself should not be called upon to
forfeit their lives for his " crimes and misdeeds." The
conventional viking, clear-eyed and purely material in
his view of life, would have stayed to brave out the
consequences. Hethin only wished " to go away somewhere a long way off, where he would not each day
have his wicked deeds cast in his teeth." His remorse
had broken him down.—" You will find it an easy
matter to slay me when I am left alive last of all! "

The motif of the Everlasting Battle is not confined

---

[1] Cf. The *Saga of Hervör and Heithrek* translated below, p. 87 ff.

to the story of Hethin and Högni. Parallels can be
found in many literatures, both ancient and modern[1].

This *tháttr* has been translated into English under
the title of *The Tale of Hogni and Hedinn* in *Three
Northern Love Stories* by W. Morris and Eiríkr
Magnússon, London, 1875.

For a full bibliography of MSS., translations, and
the general literature dealing with this saga, cf.
Islandica, Vol. v, pp. 41, 42.

THE THÁTTR OF SÖRLI

I. To the East of Vanakvisl in Asia was a country
called Asialand or Asiaheim. Its inhabitants were
called Æsir and the chief city they called Asgarth.
Othin was the name of their King, and it was a great
place for heathen sacrifices. Othin appointed Njörth
and Frey as priests. Njörth had a daughter called
Freyja who accompanied Othin and was his mistress.
There were four men in Asia called Alfregg, Dvalin,
Berling and Grer, who dwelt not far from the King's
hall, and who were so clever that they could turn
their hands to anything. Men of this kind were
called dwarfs. They dwelt in a rock, but at that time
they mixed more with men than they do now. Othin
loved Freyja very much, and she was the fairest of
all women in her day. She had a bower of her own
which was beautiful and strong, and it was said that
if the door was closed and bolted, no-one could enter
the bower against her will.

It chanced one day that Freyja went to the rock
and found it open, and the dwarfs were forging a

[1] Cf. Panzer, *Hilde-Gudrun* (Halle, 1901), *passim*; Frazer, *Pausanias's Description of Greece* (London, 1898), Vol. ii, p. 443 ff.; etc.

gold necklace, which was almost finished. Freyja
was charmed with the necklace, and the dwarfs with
Freyja. She asked them to sell it, offering gold and
silver and other costly treasures in exchange for it.
The dwarfs replied that they were not in need of
money, but each one said that he would give up his
share in the necklace....And at the end of four nights
they handed it to Freyja. She went home to her bower
and kept silence about it as if nothing had happened.

II. There was a man called Farbauti who was a
peasant and had a wife called Laufey. She was thin
and meagre, and so she was called 'Needle.' They
had no children except a son who was called Loki.
He was not a big man, but he early developed a caustic
tongue and was alert in trickery and unequalled in
that kind of cleverness which is called cunning. He
was very full of guile even in his youth, and for this
reason he was called Loki the Sly. He set off to
Othin's home in Asgarth and became his man.
Othin always had a good word for him whatever
he did, and often laid heavy tasks upon him, all
of which he performed better than could have been
expected. He also knew almost everything that
happened, and he told Othin whatever he knew.

Now it is said that Loki got to know that Freyja
had received the necklace...and this he told to Othin.
And when Othin heard of it he told Loki to fetch
him the necklace. Loki said that there was not much
hope of that, because no-one could get into Freyja's
bower against her will. Othin told him to go, and
not come back without the necklace. So Loki went
off howling, and everyone was glad that he had
got into trouble.

He went to Freyja's bower, but it was locked. He tried to get in, but could not. The weather outside was very cold and he became thoroughly chilled. Then he turned himself into a fly, and flew around all the bolts and along the whole of the woodwork, but nowhere could he find a hole big enough to enter by, right up to the gable. He found only a hole no bigger than would allow of the insertion of a needle. Through this hole he crept. And when he got inside he stared around, wondering if anyone was awake. But he found that the room was all wrapped in slumber.

Then he went in and up to Freyja's bed and found that she was wearing the necklace and that the clasp was underneath her. Loki thereupon turned himself into a flea and settled on Freyja's cheek and stung her, till she awoke and turned over and went to sleep again. Then he laid aside his flea-form, drew the necklace from her gently, opened the door and departed, carrying the necklace to Othin.

When Freyja awoke in the morning she found that the door was open, though it had not been forced, and that her lovely necklace was gone. She had a shrewd idea of the trick that had been played on her, and when she was dressed she went into the hall to King Othin, and told him that he had done ill to rob her of her trinket, and begged him to return it.

Othin replied that considering how she had come by it she should never get it back:

" —Unless you bring about a quarrel between two kings, each of whom has twenty kings subject to him; so that they shall fight under the influence of such spells and charms that as fast as they fall they shall start up again and fight on—unless there be some

Christian man so brave and so much favoured by the great good fortune of his liege lord that he shall dare to take arms and enter among the combatants and slay them. Then and not till then shall the labours of those princes be brought to an end—whoever may be the chief who is destined to free them from the oppression and toil of their disastrous lot."

Freyja agreed to this and recovered the necklace.

III. Four and twenty years after the death of Frithfrothi a King called Erling ruled over the Highlands of Norway. He had a wife and two sons, of whom the elder was called Sörli the Strong, and the younger Erlend. They were promising young men. Sörli was the stronger of the two. As soon as they were old enough they took to raiding, and fought against the viking Sindri, the son of Sveigir, the son of Haki, a sea-king in the Skerries of the Elf. There fell Sindri the viking, and with him all his host; and Erlend the son of Erling also fell in that battle. After that Sörli sailed into the Baltic and harried there, and performed so many great deeds that it would take too long to recount them all.

IV. There was a King called Halfdan who ruled Denmark; and his capital was at Roskilde. He married Hvethna the elder, and their sons were Högni and Haakon. They were distinguished for their stature, strength and ability. As soon as they were old enough they took to piracy.

Now we must return to Sörli and relate how one autumn he set sail for Denmark. King Halfdan had been intending to go to a gathering of kings. He was far advanced in years at the time when the events related here took place. He had such a fine warship

that for strength and excellence of every kind it had
no equal in all the countries of the North. It was
riding at anchor in the harbour, but King Halfdan
had gone ashore to give orders for a carousal before
starting on his voyage. And when Sörli saw the
warship, his heart was consumed with a burning
desire to possess it at all possible hazards. And indeed it is generally agreed that there never was a
greater treasure of a warship than this in all the
countries of the North, except the warships Ellithi
and Gnöth and the Long Serpent.

So he ordered his men to prepare themselves for
battle—

"For we must slay King Halfdan and seize his
warship."

A man called Sævar, his fo'c'sle-man and marshal,
made answer:

"That is not advisable, Sire, for Halfdan is a great
chief and a famous man. Moreover he has two sons
who will be certain to avenge him, for they are both
very famous men already."

"Though they be superior to the very gods," said
Sörli, "yet we shall fight just as we have done before."

They prepared for battle, and the news reached
King Halfdan. He started up and went with all his
men to his ships, and they prepared them for battle
at once. Some of Halfdan's men protested to him
that it was not advisable to fight, and suggested that
he should take to flight as the odds were too heavy
against them. The King replied that they would all
fall dead one on the top of another before he would
flee.

Both sides now prepared to give battle, and closed

forthwith in a fierce combat, the result of which was
that King Halfdan fell with all his host; and Sörli
took possession of the warship and everything on it
that was of value.

Then Sörli learned that Högni had returned from
a raiding expedition and was lying off Odinsø.
Sörli set off thither with his ships, and when they
met, he told him of the death of Halfdan, his father,
and made him an offer of reconciliation on his own
terms, suggesting also that they should become
foster-brothers; but Högni declined all his offers.
Then they joined battle, as is told in the poem dealing
with Sörli. Haakon fought very boldly and slew
Sævar, Sörli's standard-bearer and fo'c'sle-man. Then
Sörli slew Haakon, but Högni slew King Erling,
Sörli's father. After that Högni and Sörli fought
together, and Sörli went down before Högni from
weariness and wounds. And Högni afterwards
caused him to be healed of his wounds, and they
swore foster-brotherhood to one another, and both
remained true to their oaths as long as they lived.
Sörli was the first to die. He fell in the Baltic at the
hands of vikings, as is told in the poem of which he
is the subject.

And when Högni heard of Sörli's death, he went
raiding in the Baltic the same summer, and was
victorious everywhere. He became king over those
regions; and it is said that twenty kings were vassals
to King Högni and paid him tribute. Högni became
so famous on account of his great deeds and his
raiding expeditions that his name was as well known
in the north of Finland as away in Paris, and everywhere in between.

V. There was a King called Hjarrandi who ruled
over Serkland. He had a wife and a son called
Hethin, who quickly grew into a man remarkable
for his strength, stature and ability. While still a
youth he went on raiding expeditions and became a
sea-king, harrying all round Spain and Greece and
all the neighbouring kingdoms; so that he made
twenty kings pay him tribute, holding their land and
revenue as his vassals. In winter time Hethin used
to stay at home in Serkland. It is said that on one
occasion he went into a forest with his retinue. He
left his men and found himself alone in a glade where
he saw a woman, tall and fair, sitting on a throne.
She spoke to him courteously, and when he asked her
her name she said she was called Göndul. Then they
talked together. She questioned him about his
mighty deeds and he told her everything frankly
and asked her whether she knew of any king to
match himself in valour and hardihood, renown and
prowess. She replied that she knew of one who did
not fall short of him—one who had twenty kings
subject to him just as Hethin had; and she added
that his name was Högni and that he lived in the
North, in Denmark.

"I know one thing," said Hethin; "we have got
to prove which of us is the more valiant."

"It is high time for you to return to your men,"
said she; "they will be looking for you."

Then they parted. He returned to his men, and
she remained sitting there.

At the very beginning of spring, Hethin prepared
to set out. He had a warship, and three hundred and
sixty men in it, and he made for the northern part

of the world. He sailed all that summer and the following winter, and at the beginning of spring he reached Denmark.

VI. King Högni was at home at that time; and when he heard that a famous king had come to his shores, he invited him to a magnificent banquet, and Hethin accepted the invitation. And as they sat drinking, Högni asked what motive brought Hethin so far north.

Hethin replied that his object was to compete with him in contests which would make trial of their courage and daring and all their prowess and skill.

Högni said he was ready for this; and early next morning they went swimming and shooting together. They rode a-tilt, and performed feats of arms and of skill of all kinds. And in all their exploits they were so equal that no-one could distinguish which was the better of the two. After that they swore foster-brother-hood to one another, and bound themselves to share everything equally.

Hethin was young and unmarried, but Högni was somewhat older. He had married Hervör, the daughter of Hjörvarth, the son of Heithrek Ulfham. Högni had a daughter who was called Hild, and who excelled all other women in beauty and under-standing. He loved his daughter exceedingly. He had no other children.

VII. It is said that a little later Högni went on a raiding expedition while Hethin stayed behind to look after his kingdom. It chanced one day that Hethin went into a forest to pass the time. The weather was mild. He again wandered away from his men. He came upon a forest glade, and there he

saw sitting on a throne the same woman whom he had
seen before in Serkland—only now he thought her
even fairer than before. She was again the first to speak
and chattered to him gaily. She was holding a horn
with a lid to it. The King fell in love with her. She
offered him a drink and he felt thirsty, as he had
grown warm; so he took the horn and drank; and
when he had drunk, a very wonderful change came
over him, for he remembered nothing that had
happened to him previously. He then sat down and
talked to her.

She asked him if what she had said to him before
of the skill and courage of Högni had proved true
and Hethin replied that it was true enough—"for
he did not come short of me in any feat that we tried,
and so we declared ourselves a match."

"Yet you two are not equal," said she.

"And why not?" asked Hethin.

"For this reason," replied she: "Högni has
married a wife of high birth, whereas you have no
wife."

He replied: "Högni will marry me to Hild his
daughter as soon as I like to ask him, and then I shall
be as well married as he."

"Your honour will be impaired," said she, "if
you ask Högni for a marriage alliance. If, as you
profess, you lack neither courage nor valour, you
would do better to carry off Hild by force, and put
the Queen to death by taking her and laying her down
in front of the prow of your warship, and letting it
cut her in two when it is launched."

The wickedness and forgetfulness contained in the
ale which Hethin had drunk had so got the better of

him that there seemed to him to be no alternative, and he had not the slightest recollection that he and Högni were 'foster-brothers.'

Presently they parted, and Hethin went back to his men. This took place in the late summer.

Then Hethin ordered his men to get ready the warship, saying that he intended to go home to Serkland. Then he went into the ladies' bower, and took the Queen and Hild by either hand and led them out. Hild's clothes and jewels were also taken. There was no-one in the kingdom who had the courage to do anything; for they were afraid of Hethin and his men—he glowered so fiercely.

Hild asked Hethin what his intention was, and he told her. She besought him to think better of it, adding:

"My father will marry me to you if you ask him for me."

"Ask for you?" echoed Hethin; "I will never do that."

"And," she continued, "if you really must carry me off, even so my father will make it up with you. But if you do anything so wicked and unmanly as to put my mother to death, my father will never make it up with you. I have had a warning in dreams that you two will fight and slay one another. Yet I am afraid that there must be something still more terrible in store. It will be a great sorrow to me if I have to be the means of exposing my father to the ruinous effects of magic spells; nor shall I have any joy in seeing you in difficulties and toils."

Hethin replied that he cared not at all for the consequences, and that he would do as he had threatened.

"You cannot mend it now," said Hild, "because in this case you are not your own master."

Then Hethin went down to the sea-shore, and now was the warship launched. He thrust the Queen down in front of the prow, so that she perished. Hethin stepped into the warship. And when it was quite ready, he took it into his head to land alone, leaving his men behind; and he went into the same forest where he had gone before. And when he came into the glade, there he saw Göndul seated on her throne. They greeted one another cordially. Hethin told her what he had done and she expressed her approval.

She had with her the horn which she had carried before, and she offered him a drink from it. He took it and drank; and when he had drunk, sleep fell upon him, and he let his head sink into her lap. And when he had fallen asleep, she slipped away from under his head, saying:

"Now I devote both you and Högni and all your followers, and lay you under all the spells imposed by Othin."

Then Hethin awoke and saw the fleeting shadow of Göndul, but she appeared to him now to be big and black; and he recalled everything and realised how much mischief he had done. He decided now to go away somewhere a long way off, where he would not each day have his wicked deeds cast in his teeth. So he went to his ship, and made haste to free her from her moorings. A fair breeze was blowing off the land, and so he sailed away with Hild.

VIII. When Högni returned home, he learnt that Hethin had sailed away with Hild and the warship

Halfdanarnaut, leaving the dead body of the Queen in his tracks. Högni was furious and bade his men start up on the spot and sail in pursuit of Hethin. This they did, and a fair breeze sprang up. Every evening they reached the harbour from which Hethin had sailed away in the morning.

It happened one day that as Högni was making for a harbour, Hethin's sails were sighted out at sea; so Högni and his men gave chase. As a matter of fact, it is said that at this point Hethin got a head wind against him, whereas Högni had the luck to have a fair wind as before. Hethin then lay to off an island called Hoy, and there he rode at anchor. Högni quickly came alongside, and when they met, Hethin greeted him courteously.

"I must tell you, foster-brother," said Hethin, "that so great a misfortune has come upon me that no-one save you can remedy it. I have carried off your daughter and your warship, and put your wife to death, yet from no personal wickedness of my own, but rather from promptings of evil spirits and wicked spells. My wish now is that you shall have your own way entirely in this matter between yourself and me. I also offer to give up to you both Hild and the warship, and all the men and money contained in it, and to go to such distant lands that I can never return to the North nor into your sight as long as I live."

Högni replied: "Had you asked me for Hild I would have married her to you; and even in spite of your having carried her off by force we might have made up our quarrel. Now, however, since you have been guilty of such an outrage as to put the Queen to death in a most shameful manner, I certainly will not make terms with you. We will try here, on the spot, which of us is the more valiant fighter."

Hethin replied: "It would be best, if nothing less than fighting will satisfy you, that we two should measure our strength alone; for you have no quarrel with any man here save with me. There is no use in making innocent men pay for my crimes and evil deeds."

Their followers all swore with one accord that they would rather fall dead in heaps than that they two should exchange blows alone. And when Hethin saw that nothing would satisfy Högni, save that they should fight, he ordered his men to land, saying:

"I will no longer hold back from Högni, nor make excuses to avoid fighting. Let every man bear himself bravely!"

They thereupon landed and fell to fighting. Högni was full of fury, but Hethin was both dexterous with his weapons and mighty in his stroke. It is told for fact that so potent was the evil charm in the spell that even when they had cloven one another to the very shoulders, yet they started up as before and went on fighting. Hild sat in a grove and watched the battle.

This harrowing torment continued to oppress them from the time when they began to fight until Olaf Tryggvason became King of Norway. It is said to have gone on for a hundred and forty-three years, until it fell to the lot of this famous man that one of his retinue released them from their grievous calamities and tragic doom.

IX. In the first year of King Olaf's reign, it is said that he came one evening to the island of Hoy and anchored there. It was a regular occurrence in the neighbourhood of this island that watchmen disappeared every night, and no-one knew what had become of them. On this particular night it was Ivar the Gleam who kept guard. And when all the men on the ships were asleep, Ivar took the sword that Jarnskjöld had had and that Thorstein his son had given him, and all his armour, and went up on to the island. And when he had landed on the island, he saw a man coming towards him. He was very tall and covered with blood, and his face was full of sorrow. Ivar asked him his name, and he replied that he was called Hethin, the son of Hjarrandi, and that he had come of a stock in far Serkland, adding:

"I am telling you the truth when I say that the vanishing of the watchmen must be laid to the charge of me and Högni, the son of Halfdan. For we and our men have been laid under such powerful and destructive spells that we go on fighting night and day; and this has continued for many generations, while Hild, the daughter of Högni, sits and looks on. It is Othin who has laid this spell upon us; and our only hope of redemption is that a Christian man should give battle to us.—When that occurs, he whom the Christian slays shall not stand up again; and so will each one be freed from his distress. Now I would pray you that you will come to fight with us, because I know that you are a good Christian, and also that the King whom you serve is very lucky. I have a feeling too that we shall get some good from him and his men."

Ivar agreed to go with him.

Hethin was glad at that and said:

"You must take care not to encounter Högni face to face, and also not to slay me before you slay him; because no mortal man can encounter Högni face to face and slay him if I die before him, for the glance of his eye strikes terror and spares none. Therefore this is the only way: I will attack him in front and engage him in battle, while you go behind and give him his death stroke. You will find it an easy matter to slay me, when I am left alive last of all."

Then they went into the battle, and Ivar saw that all that Hethin had told him was quite true. He went behind Högni and struck him on the head, and clove his skull down to the shoulders, whereupon Högni fell down dead and never rose up again. After that he slew all the men who were fighting, and last of all he slew Hethin, which was no great task.

When he returned to the ships the day was dawning. He went to the King and told him what he had done. The King was very well pleased with his work and told him that he had had great good luck. Next day they landed and made their way to the spot where the battle had taken place; but they saw no sign of what had happened there. Yet the blood-stains on Ivar's sword were visible proofs; and never again did watchmen disappear on that coast.

After that the King went home to his realm.

INTRODUCTION TO THE SAGA OF
HROMUND GREIPSSON

In the *Saga of Thorgils and Haflithi*, ch. 10
(published in *Sturlunga Saga*, ed. by G. Vigfusson,
Vol. 1, p. 19), we are told that at a wedding held at
Reykjaholar in Iceland in 1119, "There was fun
and merriment and great festivity and all kinds of
amusements, such as dancing and wrestling and
story-telling....Although it is a matter of no great
importance, some record has been preserved of
the entertainment which was provided, and who were
the people who provided it. Stories were told which
many people now reject, and of which they disclaim
any knowledge; for it seems that many people do not
know what is true, but think some things to be true
which are really pure invention and other things to
be fictitious which are really true. Hralf of Skalmar-
nes told a story about Hröngvith the Viking and
Olaf 'the Sailors' King,' and about the rifling of the
barrow of Thrain the berserk, and about Hromund
Gripsson, and included many verses in his story.
King Sverrir used to be entertained with this story
and declared that fictitious stories like this were the
most entertaining of any. Yet there are men who
can trace their ancestry to Hromund Gripsson.
Hrolf himself had composed this story."

Among those whose ancestry was traced to
Hromund Greipsson were Ingolf and Leif, the
first Norwegian colonists of Iceland. According to

Landnámabók, 1, ch. 3, they were second cousins, and their grandfathers, who had come from Thelamörk in the south-west of Norway, were sons of Hromund. Olaf 'The Sailors' King' is mentioned also in the *Saga of Grím Lothinkinni*, ch. 3; and members of his family figure prominently in several other sagas.

These persons may actually be historical. But the fictitious element is obvious enough in many places as, for instance, in Hromund's voyage to the west. Thrain himself is vividly presented to us as "black and huge, with talons like bird's claws, all clad in glittering gold, seated on a throne, roaring loudly and blowing a fire!" This chapter is indeed a tale of

> Ghaisties and ghoulies,
> And lang-leggity beasties,
> And things that gae bump in the nicht.

The most curious features of the saga, however, are the blurred and perhaps confused reminiscences of stories and characters which form the subject of some of the Edda poems. The brothers Bild and Voli can hardly be other than corruptions of the god Balder and his avenger Váli. The name of Hromund's sword 'Mistletoe' too may be a reminiscence of the same story, though a sword of the same name is found in *Hervarar Saga* (ch. 2). Again, the account of Hromund's sojourn with Hagal, disguised as a grinding-maid, and the search made by Blind (ch. 8) are certainly reminiscences of the Edda poem *Helgakvitha Hundingsbana II* (sometimes called *Völsungakvitha*), where the same adventures are recorded in connection with the same names, except that Helgi here takes the place of Hromund.

But the most interesting case, however, is the story of Hromund's opponent Helgi the Bold and Kara (ch. 7). In this story, Helgi is said to be in the service of two kings called Hadding, and there can be little doubt that Helgi and Kara are identical with Helgi Haddingjaskati and Kara, whose adventures formed the subject of a lost poem called *Káruljóth*. This poem is referred to in the prose at the end of *Helga-kvitha Hundingsbana II*, where it is stated that they were reincarnations of Helgi Hundingsbani and Sigrún—just as the two latter were themselves reincarnations of Helgi the son of Hjörvarth and Sváva—"but that is now said to be an old wives' tale."

Chapter 4 also has a special interest of its own. Breaking into barrows was a favourite exploit of the Norsemen, no doubt for the sake of the gold which they often contained. References to the practice are very common in the sagas, e.g. *Grettissaga*, ch. 18; *Hartharsaga*, ch. 15; cf. also Saxo Grammaticus, *Dan. Hist.*, p. 200 ff., etc. The ruthlessness with which the Norsemen plundered the Irish barrows is mentioned with great indignation in the Irish Chronicles. In the *War of the Gaedhil with the Gaill*, cap. xxv, we read that certain Norsemen plundered in Ireland "until they reached Kerry; and they left not a cave there under ground that they did not explore." In the same work cap. lxix, we are told that—

Never was there a fortress, or a fastness, or a mound, or a church, or a sacred place, or a sanctuary, when it was taken by that howling, furious, loathsome crew, which was not plundered by the collectors and accumulators of that wealth. Neither was there in concealment under ground in Erin, nor in the various solitudes belonging to Fians or to Fairies, any thing that was not discovered by these foreign, wonderful Denmarkians, through paganism and idol worship.

Finally in the *Annals of Ulster* we read (sub anno 862) that

The cave of Achadh-Aldai (i.e. probably New Grange, near Dublin) and [the cave] of Knowth, and the cave of Fert-Boadan over Dowth, and the cave of the smith's wife were searched by the foreigners (i.e. Norsemen, etc.) which had not been done before.

And in England as late as 1344 Thomas of Walsingham records the slaying of the dragon that guarded a barrow, and the recovery of a great treasure of gold by the retainers of the Earl of Warrenne.

Popular imagination believed that barrows were occupied by a ghostly inhabitant 'haugbui,' who guarded the treasure. This was sometimes a dragon, as in *Beowulf*, or a reanimated corpse, as in our saga; but whatever he was, he inspired the outside world with such fear that the breaking into a grave-mound came to be regarded as a deed of the greatest courage and prowess. The 'hogboy' (*haugbui*) of Maeshowe, a barrow in the Orkneys, is still a living reality in the imaginations of the country people[1].

Unfortunately *The Saga of Hromund Greipsson* is preserved only in late paper MSS., of which none apparently are earlier than the seventeenth century.

[1] Cf. Joseph Anderson, *Scotland in Pagan Times: The Bronze and Stone Ages*, pp. 278–279 (publ. by Douglas, Edinburgh, 1886).

None of the verses of which the notice in the *Saga of Thorgils and Haflithi* speaks (cf. p. 58 above) have been preserved. There is, however, a rhymed version of the saga known as *Gríplur*, dating apparently from about the year 1400 and evidently taken from a better text than any of those which have come down to us. A short extract from these rhymed verses will be found on pp. 173–75. For a full discussion of the relationship of the *Gríplur* to the extant texts of the saga and to the later ballads, the reader is referred to Kölbing, *Beiträge zur Vergleichenden Geschichte der Romantischen Poesie und Prosa des Mittelalters* (Breslau, 1876), pp. 181–83, and to Andrews, *Studies in the Fornaldarsögur Northrlanda*[1] in *Modern Philology*, 1911, 1912.

A full bibliography of texts, translations and literature relating to this saga will be found in *Islandica*, Vol. v, p. 30.

THE SAGA OF HROMUND GREIPSSON

I. There was a King called Olaf, the son of Gnothar-Asmund, and he ruled over Garthar in Denmark, and was very famous. Two brothers, Kari and Örnulf, both mighty warriors, were entrusted with the defence of his territories. In that district there was a wealthy landowner called Greip, who had a wife called Gunnlöth, the daughter of Hrok the Black. They had nine sons whose names were

---

[1] It is pointed out by Andrews, p. 2, that the form Lara (which appears in Rafn's and Ásmundarson's editions, ch. 7) is due to a misreading. The mss. have Cara.

as follows: Hrolf, Haki, Gaut, Thröst, Angantyr, Logi, Hromund, Helgi, Hrok. They were all promising fellows, though Hromund was the finest of them. He did not know what fear was. He was blue-eyed and fair-haired; he was broad-shouldered, tall and strong, and resembled his mother's father. The King had two men called Bild and Voli. They were wicked and deceitful, but the King valued them highly.

On one occasion King Olaf was sailing eastwards with his fleet along the coast of Norway. They put in at Ulfasker, and lying to off one of the islands they began to plunder. The King bade Kari and Örnulf go up on the island and look if they could see any warships. They went up on land and saw six warships under some cliffs, one of them being a most gorgeous 'Dragon.' Kari called to the men and asked whose ships they were. One of the scoundrels on the 'Dragon' stood up and declared his name to be Hröngvith, adding:

"But what may your name be?"

Kari told him his own name and the name of his brother and added:

"You are the worst man I know and I am going to chop you into fragments."

Hröngvith replied: "For thirty-three years I have harried both summer and winter. I have fought sixty battles and been victorious every time with my sword Brynthvari, which has never grown blunt. Come here to-morrow, Kari, and I will sheathe it in your breast."

Kari said he would not fail to appear.

Hröngvith had it in his power to choose every day who was to perish by the point of his sword.

II. The brothers went back to the King and told him the news. The King gave orders to prepare for battle, and his men set to work. The hosts met and a stiff fight took place. The brothers fought bravely, Kari slaying eight or twelve men with every blow. When Hröngvith saw that, he leapt up on the King's ship, attacked Kari and thrust him through with his sword. As soon as Kari was wounded he called to the King:

"Farewell, Sire. I am going to be Othin's guest!"

Hröngvith spitted Örnulf on his spear, and when both the brothers had fallen, Hröngvith called out to the rest to surrender. Then a murmur of discontent arose in the King's host. No blade would wound Hröngvith. Now it is told that Hromund Greipsson was in the King's retinue. He took a club in his hand, fastened a long grey goat's beard on his face, drew a hood over his head, and then rushed to the fight, where he found the two brothers lying dead. He rescued the King's standard, and began to deal death among the scoundrels with his club.

Hröngvith asked who he was and if he were the father of that wretched Kari.

Hromund told him his name and said he was going to avenge the brothers:—

"Though Kari was no relative of mine, I will slay you all the same."

And thereupon he dealt Hröngvith such a blow with his club that his head was all awry afterwards.

Hröngvith said: "I have been in many battles, but I never got such a blow!"

Hromund struck another blow at Hröngvith and broke his skull. At the third stroke he died. After that all the survivors surrendered to the King, and so the battle ended.

III. Then Hromund proceeded to ransack the ship, and came upon a man prepared to offer resistance in the prow. He asked the man's name; and he replied that he was called Helgi the Bold, a brother of Hröngvith, and added: "I have no mind to sue for peace." Hromund gave orders that the wounds of Helgi the Bold should be attended to. Then he sailed away to Sweden and was entrusted with the defence of part of the country.

After that King Olaf sailed away to the British Isles with his host, as far as the Hebrides, where they landed and made a raid. There was a man dwelling hard by whose cattle had been taken and driven away by the King's men, and he was bewailing his loss piteously. Hromund went and asked him who he was.

The man replied that his name was Mani and that his home was a very little way off; and he said that they would win more honour by breaking into barrows and plundering the treasures of ghosts.

Hromund asked him to tell him if he knew anything about places of this kind.

Mani replied that he certainly did:—

"There was a berserk called Thrain, a big, strong man who was deeply versed in sorcery. He conquered Valland and was King there. He was put into a barrow with a sword, armour and great treasure; but no-one is in a hurry to go there."

Hromund asked in which direction they should sail in order to reach it, and he replied that they could reach it by sailing due south for six days.

Hromund thanked the man for his information, gave him money, and restored his cattle to him. Then they sailed away in the direction indicated by the man, and at the end of six days they saw the barrow straight in front of their ship.

IV. They went from the British Isles to Valland, and found the barrow and immediately set to work to break it open. And when six days had elapsed they came upon a trap-door in the barrow. There they beheld a big fiend, black and huge, all clad in glittering gold, and seated on a throne. He was roaring loudly and blowing a fire.

Hromund asked: "Now who will enter the barrow? Whoever does so shall have his choice of three treasures."

Voli replied: "No-one will be anxious to forfeit his life for them. There are sixty men here, and that troll will be the death of them all."

Hromund said: "Kari would have ventured on it, had he been alive," and he added—what was true enough—that even if he were let down by a rope, it would not be so bad to struggle against eight others as against Thrain.

Then Hromund climbed down by a rope.—It was during the night; and when he had got down, he gathered up a great amount of treasure and bound it to the end of the rope.

Thrain had been King of Valland in bygone days and had won all his victories by magic. He had wrought great evil; and when he was so old that he could fight no longer, he had got himself shut up alive in the barrow, and much treasure along with him.

Now Hromund saw a sword hanging up on a pillar. He took it down, girded it on, and marched up to the throne, saying:

"It is time for me to leave the barrow since there is no-one to stop me. But what ails you, old fellow? Have you not seen me gathering up your money while you sit quietly by, you hateful cur? Were you not ashamed to look on while I took your sword and necklace and ever so many more of your treasures?"

Thrain said that he cared for nothing if only he would let him sit quietly on his throne: "Formerly," he continued, "I used to be the first to fight. I must have become a great coward if I let you rob me of my wealth single handed; but I'm going to prevent your taking my treasures; you had better beware of me, dead though I am."

Then said Hromund: "Hoist yourself up on your legs, coward and weakling, and take back your sword from me if you dare."

The ghost replied: "There is no glory in attacking me with a sword when I am unarmed. I would rather try my strength in wrestling with you."

Then Hromund flung down the sword and trusted to his strength. When Thrain saw that, he took down his cauldron which he kept above him. He was by no means pleasant to watch as he blew up his fire, ready to make a meal from the cauldron. The body of the cauldron was full, and there was a big flame beneath its feet. Thrain was wearing a gold-wrought mantle. Both his hands were crooked and his finger nails were like talons.

Hromund said: "Get down off your throne, vile

wretch, now that you have been robbed of all your wealth."

Then said the ghost: "To be sure, it is high time to get on my legs, since you taunt me with lack of courage."

Day departed, and evening drew on, and it became dark in the barrow. Then the ghost began wrestling with Hromund and threw down his cauldron. Hromund put forth all his strength, and they fought so hard that rubble and stones were torn up. Then the ghost sank down on one knee, saying:

"You press me hard: you are indeed a brave fellow."

Hromund replied: "Stand up on your feet again without support. You are much weaker than Mani the peasant said."

Then Thrain turned himself into a troll, and the barrow was filled with a horrible stench: and he stuck his claws into the back of Hromund's neck, tearing the flesh from his bones down to his loins, saying:

"You need not complain if the game is rough and your body sore, for I am going to tear you limb from limb."

"I cannot imagine," cried Hromund, "how such a cat has got into this barrow!"

The ghost replied: "You must have been brought up by Gunnlöth. There are not many like you."

"It will go ill with you," said Hromund, "if you go on scratching me long."

They wrestled hard and long till everything round them shook. At last Hromund tripped him and brought him down. It had become very dark by this time.

Then said the ghost: "By guile you have overcome me and taken my sword. It was that that brought our struggle to this issue. I have lived in my barrow for a long time, brooding over my riches; but it is not wise to trust too much to one's treasures, however good they may seem. Never would I have thought that you, Mistletoe, my good sword, would do me a hurt."

Hromund then freed himself and seized the sword, and said:

"Now tell me how many men you have slain in single combat with Mistletoe."

"A hundred and forty four," said the ghost, "and I never got a scratch. I tried my skill with King Seming who was in Sweden, and he was of the opinion that it would take a long time to vanquish me."

Hromund said: "You have been a curse on men for a long time, and it will be a good deed to kill you at once."

Then he cut off the ghost's head, and burned him to ashes on the fire; and then he went out of the barrow. They asked him on what terms he and Thrain had parted, and he replied that matters had gone according to his wishes:—"For I cut off his head."

Hromund kept for himself the three treasures which he had won in the barrow—the ring, the necklace and Mistletoe; but everyone received a share of the money.

Then King Olaf sailed away to his kingdom in the north, and settled down peacefully in his own country.

V. After that Hromund grew very famous. He

was generous and popular. One day he gave to a
man called Hrok a ring of solid gold which weighed
an ounce. Voli got to know about that and slew
Hrok by night and stole the ring. And when the
King heard of it he said he would be even with Voli
some day for such a piece of villainy.

The King had two sisters, one called Dagny and
the other Svanhvit. Svanhvit was better than her
sister in every way, and had no equal between Sweden
and Halogaland.

Hromund Greipsson was at home at this time and
became friendly with Svanhvit; but he took no pre-
cautions against either Voli or Bild. On one occasion
she told Hromund that Voli and Bild were busy
slandering him to the King.

He said: "I am not afraid of any low wretch, and
I shall talk to you as long as you give me the chance."

This slander became so serious that Hromund
and his brother had to leave the King's retinue and
go home to their father.

A short time after, Svanhvit was talking to King
Olaf and said:

"Hromund, who brought us the greatest glory,
has now been banished from the royal retinue; and
in his place you retain two men who care for neither
honour nor virtue."

The King replied: "A rumour reached me that
he intended to betray you; and the sword shall part
your love."

"You have very soon forgotten," said she, "the time
when he went alone into the barrow; and no-one else
dared.—Voli and Bild will be hanged first."

And having said this, she departed hastily.

VI. Some time after this, two kings, both called Hadding, came from Sweden, and Helgi the brother of Hröngvith was with them. They challenged King Olaf to battle with them on the frozen surface of Lake Vener in the western part of the land. He preferred fighting them to abandoning his country, so he summoned Hromund and his brothers to follow him. Hromund, however, declined to go, saying that Bild and Voli were mighty fine fellows and always fought for the King.

The King departed with his host. Svanhvit was grieved at what had happened, and went to Hromund's home. Hromund welcomed her.

"Hearken now to my prayer," said she, "more favourably than you did to my brother's request, and help the King. I will give you a shield with a strap attached. Nothing can harm you while you wear this strap."

Hromund thanked her for the gift and she was comforted; so he and his eight brothers made ready to set out.

In the meantime the King and his host reached the frozen Vener, where the Swedish army was waiting for them. And in the morning, as soon as it was light enough to fight, they armed themselves on the ice, and the Swedes made a fierce onslaught. Bild was slain as soon as the battle began, but Voli was nowhere to be seen. King Olaf and King Hadding were wounded.

Hromund had pitched his tent near the side of the lake. His brothers armed themselves early in the morning; but Hromund said:

"I had a bad dream in the night; some misfortune

is in store for us, and I am not going into the battle today."

His brothers replied that it was disgraceful not to have the courage to support the King's army, when he had come for that very purpose.

They went into the battle and fought bravely, and all those of the army of the Haddings who came against them fell in heaps. A witch had come among them in the likeness of a swan. She sang and worked such powerful spells that none of Olaf's men took heed to defend themselves. Then she flew over the sons of Greip, singing loudly. Her name was Kara. At that same moment Helgi the Bold encountered the eight brothers and slew every one of them.

VII. At this point Hromund entered the battle. Helgi the Bold caught sight of him and cried:

"Here comes the man who slew my brother Hröngvith. Now you must beware of that sword of his which he got in the barrow.—You held aloof while I slew your brothers."

"You need not question my courage, Helgi," replied Hromund, "for one or other of us must fall now."

Helgi said: "Mistletoe is such a heavy weapon that you cannot use it. I will lend you another that you can manage."

"You need not taunt me with faint-heartedness," cried Hromund. "Remember the blow which I dealt Hröngvith, when I shattered his skull to atoms!"

Helgi said: "You have bound a girl's garter round your hand, Hromund. Lay aside the shield which you are carrying. It will be impossible to wound you

so long as you carry that: I am sure that you are
dependent on that girl."

Hromund could not endure these galling words,
and flung down his shield. Helgi the Bold had
always been victorious, and it was by means of magic
that he had gained his success. His mistress' name
was Kara—she who was present in the form of a
swan. Helgi brandished his sword so high over his
head that it chopped off the swan's leg. He drove the
sword down into the ground as far as the hilt, and said:

"My luck has fled now; and it was a bad business
when I missed you."

Hromund replied: "You were very unlucky,
Helgi, to be the slayer of your own mistress, and you
will have no more happiness."

Kara dropped down dead. And with the stroke
that Helgi made at Hromund, when the sword was
buried up to the hilt, the point of the sword caught
Hromund's belly and ripped it open, and Helgi
fell forward with the force of his own stroke. Hromund was not behindhand then: he struck Helgi on
the head with Mistletoe, cleaving helmet and skull
down to the shoulders, and breaking a piece out of
the sword. Then Hromund took his belt-knife and
thrust it into his belly where there was a gaping
wound, and forced back the paunch fat which was
hanging out. At the same time he stitched up the
edges of his belly with a cord, bound his clothes
firmly over it, and so continued fighting valiantly.
Men fell dead in heaps before him, and he fought
on till midnight. Then the survivors of the army of
the Haddings fled, and thereupon the battle came to
an end.

Then Hromund saw a man standing before him on the ice, and he felt convinced that he must have made the ice on the lake by spells. He perceived that it was Voli. He remarked that it was not unfitting that he should give him his deserts, and rushed at him, brandishing Mistletoe and intending to strike him. Voli blew the sword out of his hand, and it happened to light on a hole in the ice, and sank to the bottom.

Then Voli laughed and said: "You are doomed now that you have lost hold of Mistletoe."

Hromund replied: "You will die before me."

Then he leapt upon Voli and caught him up and dashed him down against the ice, so that his neckbone was broken. There lay the great sorcerer dead! But Hromund sat him down on the ice, saying:

"I did not take the girl's advice, so now I have got fourteen wounds; and in addition to that my eight brothers lie slain, and my good blade Mistletoe has fallen into the lake, and nothing will ever make up to me for the loss of my sword."

Then he went back to his tent and got some rest.

VIII. Now the King's sisters were sent for. Svanhvit examined Hromund's wound, and stitched his stomach together and tried to bring him round. She got him taken to a man called Hagal to be cured. This man's wife was very skilful, and they made him welcome and nursed him back to health. Hromund discovered that the couple were skilled in magic.

The man was a fisherman, and one day when he was fishing, he caught a pike, and on going home and cutting it open he found Hromund's sword

Mistletoe in its maw, and gave it to him. Hromund
was glad to get it and kissed the sword-hilt and
rewarded the peasant richly.

In King Hadding's army was a man called Blind
the Evil. He told the King that Hromund was alive
and was being nursed secretly in the home of the
peasant couple. The King refused to believe it,
declaring that they would not dare to conceal him;
but he ordered a search to be made. Blind and some
other men went to the dwelling of Hagal and his
wife and asked if Hromund was under their care.
The woman said he would not be found there. Blind
searched thoroughly, but did not find Hromund because the woman had hidden him under her cauldron.
Blind and his companions went away, and when they
had gone some distance Blind said:

"Our quest has not been fruitful. We must go
back again."

They did so. They went back and found the
woman. Blind told her that she was a crafty one and
had hidden Hromund under her cauldron.

"Look there then and see if you can find him,"
said she. This she said because, when she saw them
returning, she had dressed Hromund in woman's
clothes and set him to grind and turn the handmill.
The men now made search in the house and when
they came upon the girl turning the handmill they
sniffed all round the place, but she cast an un-
friendly look on the King's men, and they went away
again without finding anything.

And when they had gone away, Blind said that
the peasant's wife had made things look different
from what they were, and he had his suspicions that

it must have been Hromund who was turning the mill, dressed as a woman.—"And I see we have been deceived. We shall do no good struggling with the woman for she is more cunning than we."

They cursed her and went back home to the King, leaving matters as they stood.

IX. In the following winter Blind saw many things in a dream, and on one occasion he told his dream to the King, saying:

"I dreamed that a wolf came running from the east, and bit you and wounded you, O King."

The King said he would interpret his dream as follows:

"A King will come here from some other land, and his coming will be terrible at first; yet afterwards peace will be brought about."

And Blind said that he dreamed he saw many hawks perched on a house—"And there I espied your falcon, Sire. He was all bare and stripped of his feathers."

The King said: "A wind will come from the clouds and shake our castle."

Blind related a third dream as follows.

"I saw a herd of swine running from the south towards the King's hall and rooting up the earth with their snouts."

The King said: "That signifies the flood-tide, wet weather, and grass springing from moisture, when the sun shines on the heath."

Blind related a fourth dream:

"I thought I saw a terrible giant come hither from the east; he gave you a great wound with his teeth."

The King said: "Messengers from some King will come into my hall. They will provoke enmity and I shall be angered thereby."

"Here is a fifth dream," said Blind; "I dreamed that a terrible serpent lay coiled round Sweden."

"A splendid warship will land here, loaded with jewels," said the King.

"I had a sixth dream," said Blind; "I dreamed that dark clouds came over the land with claws and wings, and flew away with thee, O King; and I dreamed moreover that there was a serpent in the house of Hagal the peasant. He attacked people in a terrible manner. He devoured both you and me and all the men belonging to the court. Now what can that signify?"

The King said: "I have heard that there is a bear lurking not far from Hagal's dwelling. I will go and attack the bear, and it will be in a great rage."

"Next I dreamed that a dragon's form had been drawn round the King's hall, and Hromund's belt was hanging from it."

The King said: "You know that Hromund lost his sword and belt in the lake; and are you afraid of Hromund after that?"

Blind dreamed yet more dreams which he told to the King; and the King interpreted them all to his liking, and none of them according to their real significance.

But now Blind related one more dream—this time one which concerned himself.

"I dreamed that an iron ring was fixed round my neck."

The King said: "The meaning of this dream is

that you are going to be hanged; and that will be the end of both of us."

X. After that King Olaf gathered together an army and went to Sweden. Hromund accompanied him, and they took the hall of King Hadding by surprise. He was in bed in an outer chamber, and was not aware of their presence till they smashed in the door of his room. Hadding shouted to his men and asked who was disturbing the peace of the night. Hromund told him who they were.

.The King said: "You are anxious to avenge your brothers."

Hromund said that he had not come to waste words about the death of his brothers, adding—"Now you will have to pay for it and perish on the spot."

Then one of King Hadding's champions, as big as a giant, leapt up; but Hromund slew him. King Hadding covered himself up in bed and got no wound, because every time Hromund cut down at him, the sword turned and came down flat on him. Then Hromund took a club and beat King Hadding to death.

Then said Hromund: "Here I have laid low King Hadding, the most famous man I have ever seen."

The man Blind, who was also called Bavis, was bound and then hanged; and so his dream was fulfilled.

They got a quantity of gold and other booty there, and then went home. King Olaf married Svanhvit to Hromund. They were devoted to one another, and had a family of sons and daughters; they were people of great distinction in every respect. Kings and great champions sprang from their stock.

Here ends the Saga of Hromund Greipsson.

INTRODUCTION TO THE SAGA OF
HERVÖR AND HEITHREK

The *Saga of Hervör and Heithrek* is found in two vellums, the *Hauksbók* (A.M. 544), dating from c. 1325, which for convenience is usually called *H*; and MS. 2845¹ in the Royal Library at Copenhagen, dating from the fifteenth century, and generally called *R*. Besides these there are a number of paper MSS. (h) dating from the seventeenth century. According to Bugge², these have no independent value and can contribute nothing to our knowledge of the text up to the point at which the vellums break off. They are useful however as continuing the Saga beyond this point. *H* comes to an end with Gestumblindi's second riddle, while *R* breaks off just before the close of ch. 12. Beyond this point we are entirely dependent on the paper MSS. One of these (A.M. 345 written in 1694) was adopted by Rafn³ as the text for his edition of the Saga, though he gives *H* in full as an Appendix.

The MSS. differ considerably among themselves. For instance *R* omits the first chapter of the Saga, but contains *Hjalmar's Death Song*. Here, too, many of the riddles are wanting, and the order of the rest

---

¹ This MS. is identical with the one referred to as *A* in the Introduction to the *Tháttr of Nornagest* (cf. p. 11 above).

² Quoted by Heusler, *Eddica Minora* (Dortmund, 1903), p. vii.

³ *Fornaldarsögur Northrlanda* (Copenhagen, 1829), Vol. 1; *Antiquités russes* etc. (Copenhagen, 1850–2), Vol. 1.

is quite different from that of *h*. Finnur Jónsson[1] is
of the opinion that *R* is the best text throughout;
but Heusler[2], like Valdimar Ásmundarson, keeps
the order of the riddles as in *h*. Petersen[3] regards
H as the best text and follows it so far as it goes; but
when it breaks off he follows *R* mainly, although he
considers the latter MS. to be defective in many places,
"at the beginning, middle and end." He has supplied
the lacunae in it from Arn. Magn. 192, the paper
MS. which comes nearest to it, and also from others,
but with greater reservation. Valdimar Ásmundarson,
like Petersen, and no doubt influenced by him, has
followed *H* very closely in his edition of the Saga[4]
till it breaks off, and after that the paper MSS. (*h*)
most closely related to it. He does not appear to have
used *R*, and therefore omits the details of the fight on
Samsø and *Hjalmar's Death Song*. Ásmundarson's
version has been followed closely in the translation
given below, but one or two interesting passages
omitted by *H* have been translated separately (see
Appendix on pp. 144–150) from the text printed from
R in Wimmer's *Oldnordisk Læsebog*[5] and from some
short excerpts from *h* printed at the close of Petersen's edition of the Saga.

For a full bibliography of the texts, translations,
and literature dealing with this saga the reader is
referred to *Islandica*, Vol. v, pp. 22–26.

[1] *Oldnorske og Oldislandske Litteraturs Historie*, Vol. ii, p. 839 f.

[2] *Eddica Minora*, pp. 106–120.

[3] Cf. *Forord* to N. M. Petersen's edition of *Hervarar Saga ok
Heithreks Konungs* (published by the 'Nordiske Literatur-Samfund,'
Copenhagen, 1847).

[4] See *Fornaldarsögur Northrlanda* (Reykjavík, 1891), Vol. i,
pp. 309–360.   [5] Copenhagen, 4th edition, 1889.

In this saga we have what appears to be the history of a certain family for more than four generations. From the point of view of construction, the story can hardly be regarded as a success. Yet it contains scenes at least equal to any others which can be found among sagas of this kind. It also embodies a considerable amount of poetry which is not found elsewhere. Some of this is of high merit, and one piece, dealing with the battle between the Huns and the Goths, is evidently of great antiquity.

The Saga opens in a purely mythical milieu—with Guthmund in Glasisvellir, to whom we have already had reference in the story of Nornagest. Next we have a typical story of the Viking Age—the adventures of the sons of Arngrim and their fight on Samsø. This story is known to us from other sources, the earliest being the poem *Hyndluljôth* (str. 24), which according to Finnur Jónsson[1] cannot be later in date than the latter part of the tenth century, though Mogk[2] is inclined to doubt this. Other references occur in the *Saga of Örvar-Odd*, Saxo's *Danish History*, the later ballads translated below, etc.

We then pass on to the account of Hervör, the daughter of Angantyr (which is only found here and in the ballads), and the striking poem in which she is represented as visiting her father's grave-mound to obtain his sword.

The next and longest section contains the life of Hervör's son Heithrek, which is peculiar to this saga and which in its earlier part likewise seems to be

---

[1] *Oldnorske og Oldislandske Litteraturs Historie,* Vol. i, p. 201.

[2] *Geschichte der Norwegisch-Isländischen Literatur* (Strassburg, 1904), p. 605.

a story of the Viking Age. Towards the end, however, it gradually dawns upon us that there has been
an unconscious change of scene, and that Heithrek,
instead of being a Viking prince of the Northern
coasts, is now represented as a King of the Goths,
somewhere in the East of Europe—apparently in
the neighbourhood of the Dnieper. In the last
section of the story, dealing with the adventures of
Angantyr and Hlöth, the sons of Heithrek, there
is no longer any reminiscence of the Viking Age or
the North of Europe. Here we are away back among
the Goths and Huns in the fifth or the latter part of
the fourth century.

Throughout this strange concatenation of scenes
a connecting link is afforded by the magic flaming
sword, which is handed on from generation to
generation, and which can never be sheathed without
having dealt a death wound.

It is abundantly clear that the latter part of the
story is of a totally different origin from the first part,
and in reality many centuries earlier. The prose here
is for the most part little more than a paraphrase of
the poem, which probably has its roots in poetry of
the Gothic period. But how this story came to be
joined on to a narrative of the Viking Age is far from
clear.

It is also interesting to note that some of the
characters in the saga are repetitions of one another.
At all events what is said about Hervör the daughter
of Heithrek in the latter part of the story bears a
strong resemblance to the description of the more
prominent Hervör, the daughter of Angantyr, in
the first part.

Three poems of considerable length are preserved in the story. The Riddles of Gestumblindi, though somewhat tedious as a whole, afford a better specimen of this type of composition than is to be found elsewhere in early Norse literature. They cannot fail to be of considerable interest to anyone who studies the Anglo-Saxon Riddles, though unlike the latter they are wholly Teutonic in spirit and form. Direct Latin influence appears to be entirely absent.

Gestumblindi's Riddles, while they belong essentially to popular literature, yet contain many arresting phrases which show a minute observation of nature. They illustrate the condensed, proverbial type of wisdom that prevails in a primitive state of society, as well as its keen interest and delight in the little things of life. They can hardly be called literature as we understand the term; they are rather the stuff of which literature is made. But though it is a far cry from these little nature verses to the more beautiful and more ambitious nature poems of Burns and Tennyson, yet Gestumblindi's loving interest in "every creature of earth" surprised even King Heithrek into comment. The keen and whimsical observation that noted that even a spider is a "marvel" and that it "carries its knees higher than its body" is the same spirit that inspired a poem to the

Wee sleekit, cowrin', tim'rous beastie.

The poet who noticed that water falling as hail on rock looks *white* by contrast, yet forms little *black* circles when it falls into the sand as rain, had much in common with one who noticed that rock and sand yield opposite sounds when struck by the same object—

> Low on the sand and loud on the stone
> The last wheel echoed away.

But though these things are pleasing in themselves, they are, of course, slight. Gestumblindi cannot rise to the heights of true poetry reached by Burns or Tennyson.

Besides the Riddles, this saga has preserved for us two far finer poems—in fact two of the finest Norse poems that we possess—the dialogue between Hervör and Angantyr at the Barrows of Samsø, and the narrative of the great battle between the Goths and the Huns, the *Chevy Chase* of the North. The ruthlessness and barbaric splendour of the Hunnish leaders, the cruelty and the poetry of warfare a thousand years ago, are here vividly depicted in Norse verse at its simplest and best.

We may notice too the little vignettes that appear from time to time both in the poetry itself and in the prose narrative, some of which is evidently derived from lost verses.—Hervör standing at sunrise on the summit of the tower and looking southward towards the forest; Angantyr marshalling his men for battle and remarking drily that there used to be more of them when mead drinking was in question; great clouds of dust rolling over the plain, through which glittered white corslet and golden helmet, as the Hunnish host came riding on.

The dialogue between Hervör and Angantyr, despite a certain melodramatic element in the setting, is treated with great delicacy and poetic feeling, and an atmosphere of terror and mystery pervades the

whole poem. The midnight scene in the eerie and
deserted burial-ground, the lurid flickering of the
grave fires along the lonely beach, the tombs opening
one by one as the corpses start to life—all these work
on the imagination and create an atmosphere of
dread. The poet understood the technique of pre-
senting the supernatural, and he is deliberately vague
and suggestive. Much more is implied than is stated,
and much is left to the imagination.

The greatest charm of the poem, however, lies
in the sympathetic treatment of Hervör. The Hervör
of the prose narrative is perfectly consistent with the
Hervör of the poem, but at the same time the poem
—which is probably more than a century older than
the saga—would lead us to conclude that her character was not correctly understood by the writer of
the saga. Obviously unsympathetic, he denounces
her with an indignation which would have made the
writer of the poem smile.

"She grew up to be a beautiful girl...but as soon
as she could do anything it was oftener harm than
good; and when she had been checked she escaped
to the woods....And when the Earl heard of it he
had her caught and brought home."

The picture which the poem presents to us is
that of a high-spirited girl, headstrong and impulsive,
not unlike Brynhild in the Völsung story. When
she goes to the barrows, every nerve is strung
up to gain the treasure that has fired her imagination:

> What care I though the death-fires blaze,
> They sink and tremble before my gaze,
>   They quiver out and die!

But a reaction comes when she holds the sword
in her hands at last:

> Surely in terror I drew my breath
> Between the worlds of life and death
>   When the grave fires girt me round.

Surveying the saga as a whole, perhaps the most
striking feature is its extraordinary diversity of
interest. It would be difficult to find elsewhere in
Norse literature—or indeed perhaps in any literature
—so great a variety of subjects and of literary forms
brought together within such narrow limits.

Of the poems contained in the saga, the first is
romantic, the second gnomic, the third heroic—
and the prose narrative itself is not less varied in
character. The conclusion of the saga appears to be
purely historical; indeed it is generally regarded
as one of the most important authorities for early
Swedish history. Elsewhere also historical elements
are probably not wanting, but they are interwoven
in a network of romance and folklore. Thus whoever King Heithrek may have been, the part which
he has come to play in the saga is chiefly that of
linking together a number of folk-tales and illus-
trating popular saws. As regards chronology, the
war described in ch. 12–15 must belong to a period
nearly seven centuries before the incidents related
at the close of the saga. Still more strange is the
fact that the victor in this war, the younger Angantyr,
would seem to have lived some four or five centuries
before his great grandfather and namesake who
perished at Samsø—if indeed the latter story rests
on any genuine tradition. In spite of these and

similar inconsistencies, however, the saga is on
the whole perhaps the most attractive of all the
Fornaldarsögur.

THE SAGA OF HERVÖR AND HEITHREK

Here begins the Saga of King Heithrek the Wise.

I. It is said that in the days of old the northern part
of Finnmark was called Jötunheimar, and that there
was a country called Ymisland to the south between
it and Halogaland. These lands were then the home
of many giants and half-giants; for there was a great
intermixture of races at that time, because the giants
took wives from among the people of Ymisland.

There was a king in Jötunheimar called Guthmund.
He was a mighty man among the heathen. He dwelt
at a place called Grund in the region of Glasisvellir.
He was wise and mighty. He and his men lived for
many generations, and so heathen men believed that
the fields of immortality lay in his realm; and whoever
went there cast off sickness or old age and became
immortal.

After Guthmund's death, people worshipped him
and called him their god. His son's name was
Höfund. He had second sight and was wise of
understanding, and was judge of all suits throughout
the neighbouring kingdoms. He never gave an un-
just judgment, and no-one dared violate his decision.

There was a man called Hergrim who was a giant
dwelling in the rocks. He carried off from Ymisland
Ama the daughter of Ymir, and afterwards married
her. Their son Thorgrim Halftroll took from

Jötunheimar Ögn Alfasprengi, and afterwards married her. Their son was called Grim. She had been betrothed to Starkath Aludreng, who had eight hands; but she was carried off while he was away to the north of Elivagar. When he came home he slew Hergrim in single combat; but Ögn ran herself through with a sword rather than marry Starkath. After that Starkath carried off Alfhild the daughter of King Alf from Alfheimar, but he was afterwards slain by Thor.

Then Alfhild went to her kinsfolk, and Grim was with her there till he went raiding and became a great warrior. He married Bauggerth the daughter of Starkath Aludreng and set up his dwelling on an island off Halogaland called Bolm. He was called Ey-grim Bolm. His son by Bauggerth was called Arngrim the Berserk, who afterwards lived in Bolm and was a very famous man.

II. There was a King called Sigrlami who was said to be a son of Othin. His son Svafrlami succeeded to the kingdom after his father and was a very great warrior. One day as the King rode a-hunting he got separated from his men, and at sunset he came upon a big stone and two dwarfs beside it. The King banned them with his graven sword from entering the stone. The dwarfs begged him to spare their lives.

The King said: "What are your names?"

One of them said his name was Dvalin and the other Dulin.

The King said: "As you are the most cunning of all dwarfs you must make me a sword, the best you can. The hilt and the grip must be of gold, and it must cut iron as easily as if it were cloth and never rust; and it must bring victory to whoever uses it in battle and single combat."

They agreed to this, and the King rode away home.

And when the appointed day came, the King rode to the stone. The dwarfs were outside, and they handed to the King a sword which was very beautiful.

But as Dvalin was standing in the doorway of the stone he said:

"Your sword, Svafrlami, will be the death of a man every time it is drawn; and moreover it will be the instrument of three pieces of villainy; and to you yourself also it shall bring death."

Then the King struck at the dwarfs with the sword. But they sprang into the stone, and the sword came down on it—sinking so deep that both the ridges of the blade were hidden; for the door into the stone closed as they disappeared. The King called the sword 'Tyrfing,' and ever afterwards he carried it in battle and single combat, and was always victorious.

The King had a daughter who was called Eyfura, an exceedingly beautiful and clever girl.

At that time Arngrim was raiding among the Perms in the Baltic. He raided the Kingdom of King Svafrlami and fought against him. They met face to face, and King Svafrlami struck at Arngrim who parried the blow with his shield; but the lower part of the shield was cut away and the sword plunged into the earth. Then Arngrim struck off the King's hand, so that he had to let Tyrfing fall. Arngrim caught up Tyrfing and cut down first the King, and then many others. He took great booty there, and carried off Eyfura, the King's daughter and took her to his home in Bolm.

By her he had twelve sons. The eldest was Angantyr, then Hervarth, then Hjörvarth, Sæming and
Hrani, Brami, Barri, Reifnir, Tind and Bui, and the
two Haddings who only did one man's work between
them, because they were twins and the youngest of the
family; whereas Angantyr, who was a head taller than
other men, did the work of two. They were all berserks, and were unequalled in strength and courage.
Even when they went marauding there were never
more than just the twelve brothers on one ship.
They raided far and wide in many lands, and had
much success and won great renown. Angantyr had
Tyrfing, and Sæming Mistletoe, Hervarth had
Hrotti, and each of the others possessed a sword
famous in single combat. And it was their custom,
when they had only their own men with them, to
land when they felt the berserks' fury coming upon
them, and wrestle with trees or great rocks; for they
had been known to slay their own men and disable
their ship. Great tales were told about them and they
became very famous.

III. One Yule Eve at Bolm, Angantyr made a vow
over the pledge cup, as the custom then was, that he
would wed Ingibjörg the daughter of King Yngvi
of Upsala—the cleverest and most beautiful maiden
in all the Northlands—or perish in the attempt and
marry no-one else. No more of their vows are recorded.

Tyrfing had this characteristic, that whenever it
was unsheathed it shone like a sunbeam, even in the
dark, and could only be sheathed with human blood
still warm upon it. Never did he whose blood was
shed by Tyrfing live to see another day. It is very
famous in all stories of the olden days.

Next summer the brothers went to Upsala in Sweden, and when they had entered the hall, Angantyr told the King his vow and that he intended to wed his daughter.

Everybody in the hall listened. Angantyr asked the King to declare what was to be the result of their errand, whereupon Hjalmar the stout-hearted rose from the table, and addressed the King:

"Call to mind, Sire, how much honour I have won for you since I came into your kingdom, and how many times I have risked my life for you. In return for these my services I beg that you will give me your daughter in marriage. And moreover I consider myself more deserving a favourable answer than these berserks, who do harm to everyone."

The King pondered over the matter, and found it difficult to decide the question in such a way as to give rise to as little trouble as possible; and he answered at last:

"My wish is that Ingibjörg should choose for herself the husband she prefers."

She replied: "If you want to marry me to anyone, then I would rather have a man whose good qualities I know already than one of whom I have only known by hearsay, and nothing but evil at that."

Angantyr said: "I will not bandy words with you; for I can see that you love Hjalmar. But as for you, Hjalmar, come south to Samsø and meet me in single combat. If you do not appear next midsummer you will be a coward in the eyes of all men."

Hjalmar said that he would not fail to come and fight, and the sons of Arngrim went home to their

father and told him what had happened. He replied
that this was the first time he had ever felt any
anxiety on their behalf.

They spent the winter at home, and in the spring
made ready to start, going first to Earl Bjartmar, where
a feast was made for them. And during the evening
Angantyr asked the Earl for the hand of his daughter,
and in this as in the rest they got their wish. The
wedding took place, and afterwards the sons of
Arngrim prepared to set out. But the night before
they left, Angantyr had a dream which he related to
the Earl:

I dreamed that I and my brothers were in Samsø.
We found many birds there and killed all that we
saw. Then I dreamed that as we were setting out
again upon the island, two eagles flew towards us.
I went against one and we had a stiff encounter; and
at last we sank down and had no strength left in us.
But the other eagle fought with my eleven brothers
and overcame them all."

The Earl said: "The death of mighty men has
been revealed to you in this dream."

Then Angantyr and his brothers went away and
came to Samsø, and went ashore to look for Hjalmar;
and the story of their adventures there is related in
the *Saga of Örvar-Odd*. First they came to Munarvagar, where they slew all the men from the two ships
of Hjalmar and Odd; and afterwards they went
ashore and encountered Hjalmar and Odd themselves on the island. Odd slew Angantyr's eleven
brothers, and Hjalmar slew Angantyr, and afterwards died there himself of his wounds.

Then Odd had all the rest of them placed in great

barrows with all their weapons; but Hjalmar's body
he took home to Sweden. And when Ingibjörg the
King's daughter saw Hjalmar's body, she fell down
dead, and they were both laid together in one barrow
at Upsala.

IV. The story goes on to say that a girl was
born to the daughter of Earl Bjartmar. Everyone
advised exposing the child, saying that if she resembled her father's kinsmen she would not have a
womanly disposition. The Earl, however, had her
sprinkled with water; and he brought her up, and
called her Hervör, saying that the line of Arngrim's
sons would not be extinguished if she were left
alive.

She grew up to be a beautiful girl. She was tall
and strong, and trained herself in the use of bow,
shield and sword. But as soon as she could do anything it was oftener harm than good; and when she
had been checked she ran away to the woods and
killed people to provide herself with money. And
when the Earl heard of it, he had her caught and
brought home, where she remained for a time.

One day she went to the Earl and said: "I want
to go away because I am not happy here."

A little while after she departed alone, dressed
and armed like a man, and joined some vikings and
stayed with them for a time, calling herself Hervarth.
Shortly afterwards the chief of the vikings died, and
Hervarth took command of the band.

One day when they sailed to Samsø, Hervarth
landed; but her men would not follow her, saying
that it was not safe for anyone to be out of doors
there by night. Hervarth declared that there was

likely to be much treasure in the barrows. She
landed on the island towards sunset, but they lay
off in Munarvagar. She met a shepherd boy and
asked him for information.

He said: "You are a stranger to the island; but
come home with me, for it is unsafe for anyone to be
out of doors here after sunset; and I am in a hurry to
get home."

Hervarth replied: "Tell me where are 'Hjörvarth's Barrows,' as they are called."

"You must surely be mad," replied the boy, "if
you want to explore by night what no-one dare visit
at mid-day. Burning flame plays over them as soon
as the sun has set."

But Hervarth insisted that she would visit the
barrows—whereupon the shepherd said:

"I see that you are a brave man though not a wise
one, so I will give you my necklace if you will come
home with me."

But Hervarth replied: "Even if you give me all
you have you will not hold me back."

And when the sun had set, loud rumblings were
heard all over the island, and flames leapt out of the
barrows. Then the shepherd grew frightened and
took to his heels and ran to the wood as fast as he
could, without once looking back. Here is a poem
giving an account of his talk with Hervör:

> Driving his flocks at the fall of day,
> In Munarvagar along the bay,
>   A shepherd met a maid.—
> "Who comes to our island here alone?
> Haste to seek shelter, the day is done,
>   The light will quickly fade."

"I will not seek for a resting place:
A stranger am I to the island race.—
            But tell me quick I pray,
Ere thou goest hence, if I may descry
Where the tombs of the children of Arngrim lie:
            O tell me, where are they?"

"Forbear from such questions utterly!
Foolish and rash must thou surely be,
            And in a desperate plight!
Let us haste from these horrors as fast as we can,
For abroad it is ghastly for children of men
            To wander about in the night."

"My necklace of gold is the price I intend
To pay for thy guidance; for I am the friend
            Of vikings, and will not be stayed."
"No treasures so costly, nor rings of red gold
Shall take me their thrall, or my footsteps withhold,
            That thereby my flight be gainsaid.

"Foolish is he who comes here alone
In the fearsome dark when the sun has gone
            And the flames are mounting high;—
When earth and fen are alike ablaze,
And tombs burst open before thy gaze:
            O faster let us hie!"

"Let us never heed for the snorting blaze,
Nor fear, though over the island ways
            Dart tongues of living light.
Let us not lightly give way to fear
Of the noble warriors buried here,
            But talk with them tonight."

But the shepherd lad fled fast away,
Nor stayed to hear what the youth would say,
            But into the forest sped;
While in Hervör's breast rose proud and high
Her hard-knit heart, as she saw near by
            The dwellings of the dead.

She could now see the fires of the barrows and the
ghosts standing outside; and she approached the
barrows fearlessly and passed through the fires as if
they had been merely smoke, until she reached the
barrow of the berserks. Then she cried:

V. Awaken, Angantyr, hearken to me!
  The only daughter of Tofa and thee
      Is here and bids thee awake!
  Give me from out the barrow's shade
  The keen-edged sword which the dwarfs once made
      For Svafrlami's sake.

Hervarth, Hjörvarth, Angantyr,
And Hrani, under the tree-roots here,
      I bid you now appear;—
Clad in harness and coat of mail,
With shield and broadsword of biting steel,
      Helmet and reddened spear!

The sons of Arngrim are changed indeed
To heaps of dust, and Eyfura's seed
      Has crumbled into mould.—
In Munarvagar will no one speak
To her who has come thus far to seek
      Discourse with the men of old?

Hervarth, Hjörvarth, Angantyr
And Hrani, great be your torment here
      If ye will not hear my words.
Give me the blade that Dvalin made;
It is ill becoming the ghostly dead
      To keep such costly swords!

In your tortured ribs shall my curses bring
A maddening itch and a frenzied sting,
      Till ye writhe in agonies,
As if ye were laid to your final rest
Where the ants are swarming within their nest,
      And revelling in your thighs!

Then answered Angantyr:
>O Hervör, daughter, why dost thou call
>Words full of cursing upon us all?
>>Thou goest to meet thy doom!
>Mad art thou grown, and thy wits are fled;
>Thy mind is astray, that thou wak'st the dead
>>—The dwellers in the tomb.

>No father buried me where I lie,
>Nor other kinsman[1]...
>The only two who remained unslain
>Laid hold on Tyrfing, but now again
>>One only possesses the sword.

She answered:
>Nought save the truth shalt thou tell to me!
>May the ancient gods deal ill with thee
>>If thou harbour Tyrfing there!
>Thine only daughter am I, and yet
>Unwilling thou art that I should get
>>That which belongs to thine heir!

It now seemed as if the barrows, which had opened,
were surrounded with an unbroken ring of flame.
Then Angantyr cried:
>The barrows are opening! Before thy gaze
>The round of the island is all ablaze,
>>And the gate of Hell stands wide.
>There are spectres abroad that are ghastly to see.
>Return, little maiden, right hastily
>>To thy ship that waits on the tide.

She replied:
>No funeral fire that burns by night
>Can make me tremble with affright,
>>Or fear of awful doom.
>Thy daughter's heart can know no fear,
>Though a ghost before her should appear
>>In the doorway of the tomb.

[1] Two lines are missing from the MS. at this point.

Angantyr:

> O Hervör, Hervör, hearken to me!
> Nought save the truth will I tell to thee
> > That will surely come about!
> Believe me, maiden, Tyrfing will be
> A curse upon all thy progeny
> > Till thy race be blotted out.
>
> A son shalt thou bear, as I prophesy,
> Who shall fight with Tyrfing mightily,
> > And trust to Tyrfing's might.
> I tell thee Heithrek shall be his name,
> The noblest man and of greatest fame
> > Of all under Heaven's light.

Hervör:

> On all you dead this curse I cry:—
> Mouldering and rotting shall ye lie
> > With the spirits in the tomb!
> Out of the barrow, Angantyr,
> Give me the keen-edged Tyrfing here,
> > The sword called 'Hjalmar's Doom'!

Angantyr:

> Surely unlike to a mortal thou
> To wander about from howe to howe,
> > And stand in the doorway here!
> In the horror of night-time, my little maid,
> Thou comest with helmet and byrnie and blade,
> > And shakest thy graven spear!

Hervör:

> A mortal maiden is she who comes,
> Arousing the corpses within their tombs,
> > And will not be denied:—
> Give me from out the barrow's shade
> The keen-edged sword that the dwarf-folk made,
> > Which it ill becomes thee to hide!

Angantyr:

    The sword that the death-stroke to Hjalmar gave
    Lies under my shoulders within the grave,
        And wrapped about with flame.
    But that maiden lives not in any land
    Who dare grasp the weapon within her hand
        For any hope of fame.

Hervör:

    There lives, O Angantyr, a maid
    Who yearns to handle the keen-edged blade,
        And such a maid am I!
    And what care I though the tomb fires blaze!
    They sink and tremble before my gaze,
        They quiver out and die!

Angantyr:

    O Hervör, 'tis folly and madness dire
    To rush wide-eyed through the flaming fire
        With courage undismayed.
    Rather by far will I give to thee
    The accursed sword, though unwillingly,
        My little, tender maid.

Hervör:

    O son of the vikings, well hast thou done
    In giving me Tyrfing from out the tomb;
        And happier am I today
    That I now grasp Tyrfing within my hands
    Than if I were queen of the broad Northlands,
        And conqueror of Noroway.

Angantyr:

    Vain is thy rapture, my luckless maid!
    Thy hopes are false. All too soon will fade
        The flush of joy from thy face.
    Try, child, to listen; I am warning thee!—
    This sword is the sword of destiny,
        The destroyer of all thy race!

Hervör:

> Away, away to my 'ocean-steed'!
> The daughter of princes is glad indeed,
>> O glad at heart today!
> And what care I for the destiny
> Of children as yet undreamed by me?—
>> Let them quarrel as they may!

Angantyr:

> Thou shalt have and enjoy without sorrow or pain
> The blade which proved to be Hjalmar's bane,
>> If thou draw it not from its sheath.
> Worse than a plague is this cursed thing.
> Touch not its edges, for poisons cling
>> Above it and beneath.

> Farewell, yet fain would I give to thee
> The life that has passed from my brothers and me,
>> O daughter, 'tis truth I say!
> —The strength and vigour and hardihood,
> —All that we had that was great and good,
>> That has vanished and passed away!

Hervör:

> Farewell, farewell to all you dead!
> Farewell! I would that I were sped!
>> Farewell all you in the mound!...
> Surely in terror I drew my breath
> Between the Worlds of Life and Death
>> When the grave fires girt me round!

Then she returned towards her ships; but when
dawn came, she saw that they had departed. The
vikings had been scared by the rumblings and the
flames on the island. She got a ship to carry her
away; but nothing is told of her voyage till she came
to Guthmund in Glasisvellir, where she remained all
through the winter, still calling herself Hervarth.

VI. One day Guthmund was playing chess, and when the game was almost up, he asked if anyone could advise him as to his moves. So Hervarth went up to him and began to direct his moves; and it was not long before Guthmund began to win. Then somebody took up Tyrfing and drew it. When Hervarth saw this, he snatched the sword out of his hands, and slew him, and then left the room. They wanted to rush out in pursuit, but Guthmund said:

"Don't stir—you will not be avenged on the man so easily as you think, for you don't know who he is. This woman-man will cost you dear before you take his life."

After that Hervör spent a long time in piracy and had great success. And when she grew tired of that she went home to the Earl, her mother's father. There she behaved like other girls, working at her embroidery and fine needlework.

Höfund, the son of Guthmund, heard of this and went and asked for the hand of Hervör, and was accepted; and he took her home.

Höfund was a very wise man and so just in his judgments that he never swerved from giving a correct decision, whether the persons involved were natives or foreigners. And it is from him that the 'höfund' or judge of law-suits takes his name in every realm.

He and Hervör had two sons. One was called Angantyr, the other Heithrek. They were both big strong men—sensible and handsome. Angantyr resembled his father in character and was kindly disposed towards everyone. Höfund loved him very much, as indeed did everybody. But however much good he did, Heithrek did still more evil. He was Hervör's favourite. His foster-father was called Gizur.

One day Höfund held a feast and invited all the chief men in his kingdom except Heithrek. This greatly displeased him, but he put in an appearance all the same, declaring that he would do them some mischief. And when he entered the hall, Angantyr rose and went to meet him and invited him to sit beside him. Heithrek was not cheerful, but he sat till late in the evening after Angantyr had gone; and then he turned to the men who sat on either side of him and worked upon them by his conversation in such a way that they became infuriated with each other. But when Angantyr came back he told them to be quiet. And when Angantyr went out a second time, Heithrek reminded them of his words, and worked upon them to such an extent that one of them struck the other. Then Angantyr returned and persuaded them to keep the peace till morning. And the third time Angantyr went away, Heithrek asked the man who had been struck why he had not the courage to avenge himself. And so effective did his persuasion prove that he who had been struck sprang up and slew his companion. When Angantyr returned, he was displeased at what had taken place. And when Höfund heard of it, he told Heithrek that he must either leave his kingdom or forfeit his life.

So Heithrek went out, and his brother with him. Then his mother came up and gave him Tyrfing. And Heithrek said to her:

"I don't know when I shall be able to show as much difference in my treatment of my father and

mother as they do in their treatment of me. My
father proclaims me an outlaw while my mother has
given me Tyrfing, which is of more account to me
than a great territory. But I shall do that very thing
that will most distress my father."

He then drew the sword, which gleamed and
flashed brilliantly, and then he got into a great rage
and showed the berserk's fury coming upon him.
The two brothers were alone. Now since Tyrfing
had to be the death of a man every time it was drawn,
Heithrek dealt his brother his death-blow. Höfund
was told of it, and Heithrek escaped at once to the
woods. Höfund had a funeral feast made for his
son Angantyr, and he was lamented by everybody.

Heithrek got little joy of his deed and lived in the
woods for a long time, shooting deer and bears for
food. And when he came to think over his position,
he reflected that there would be but a poor tale to
tell if no-one was to know what had become of him;
and it occurred to him that he could even yet become
a man famous for deeds of prowess like his ancestors
before him. So he went home and sought out his
mother and begged her to ask his father to give him
some sound advice before they parted. She went to
Höfund and asked him to give their son sound
advice. Höfund replied that he would give him a
little, but added that it would turn out to his dis-
advantage nevertheless; he said however that he
would not ignore his request:

"In the first place he must not aid a man who has
slain his liege lord. Secondly, he must not protect a
man who has slain one of his comrades. Thirdly, his
wife ought not to be always leaving home to visit her

relatives. Fourthly, he ought not to stay out late with his sweetheart. Fifthly, he should not ride his best horse when he is in a hurry. Sixthly, he ought not to bring up the child of a man in a better position than himself. Seventhly, let him always be cheerful towards one who comes for hospitality. Eighthly, he should never lay Tyrfing on the ground.—Yet he will not get any benefit from this advice."

His mother repeated these maxims to him.

Heithrek replied: "This advice must have been given me in a spiteful spirit. It will not be of any use to me."

His mother gave him a mark of gold at parting, and bade him always bear in mind how sharp his sword was, and how great renown had been won by everyone who had borne it—what great protection its sharp edges afforded to him who wielded it in battle or single combat, and what great success it always had.—Then they parted.

He went on his way; and when he had gone a short distance he came upon some men who were leading a man in bonds. Heithrek asked what the man had done, and they replied that he had betrayed his liege lord. He asked if they would accept money as his ransom, and they said that they were willing to do so. He ransomed the man for half his gold mark.

The man then offered to serve him, but Heithrek replied:

"You would not be faithful to a stranger like me, seeing that you betrayed your liege lord to whom you owed many benefits."

Shortly after he again came upon some men, of

whom one was in bonds. He asked what this man had done, and they replied that he had murdered one of his comrades. He freed him with the other half of his gold mark. This man also offered to serve him, but Heithrek declined.

After that he went on his way till he came to Reithgotaland, where he went to the King who ruled there. His name was Harold, and he was an old man at the time. Heithrek remained for a time with the King, who gave him a cordial welcome.

VII. There were two Earls who had plundered the kingdom of King Harold and made it subject to them, and because he was old he paid them tribute every year. Heithrek grew intimate with the King, and eventually it came about that he became the commander of his army and betook himself to raiding, and soon made himself famous for his victories. He proceeded to make war on the Earls who had subdued King Harold's kingdom, and a stiff fight took place between them. Heithrek fought with Tyrfing and, as in the past, no-one could withstand it, for it cut through steel as easily as cloth; and the result was that he slew both the Earls and put all their army to flight. He then went throughout the kingdom and brought it under King Harold and took hostages, and then returned home. And as a mark of great honour, King Harold went himself to meet him, and he acquired great fame from this. The King gave him his daughter Helga in marriage and with her half his kingdom. Heithrek had the defence of the whole realm in his hands; and this arrangement lasted for a time.

King Harold had a son in his old age. Heithrek

also had a son, who was called Angantyr. Presently
a great famine began in Reithgotaland (which is
now called Jutland) and it threatened to destroy all
the inhabitants. So they tried divination, and the
answer was that there would be no plenty in Reithgotaland until the noblest boy in the land had been
sacrificed. Heithrek said that that was King Harold's
son, but the King declared that Heithrek's son was
the noblest; and there was no escape from this
dilemma save by referring it to Höfund, whose
decisions were always just.

Thereupon Heithrek went to visit his father, who
made him welcome. He asked his father's decision
about this question. Höfund pronounced Heithrek's
son to be the noblest in that land.

"What compensation do you adjudge to me for
my loss?" asked Heithrek.

"You shall claim for yourself in compensation
every second man in the retinue of King Harold.
Beyond that there is no need to give you advice,
considering your character and the army that you
have under you."

Then Heithrek went back and summoned a
meeting, and told them his father's opinion:

"He decided that it was my son who must be
sacrificed; and as compensation to me he adjudged
to me every second man of those who are with King
Harold, and I want you to swear an oath that this
shall be done."

And they did so. Then the people demanded that
he should give up his son and get them a better
harvest. Heithrek then talked with his men after
the force had been divided, and demanded fresh

oaths of allegiance from them. These they gave, swearing to follow him whether at home or abroad, for whatever purpose he wished.

Then said he: "It appears to me that Othin will have been well compensated for one boy if he gets in place of him King Harold and his son and all his host!"

He then bade his men raise his standard and make an attack on King Harold and slay him and all his host, declaring that he was giving this host to Othin instead of his own son. He caused the altars to be reddened with the blood of King Harold and his son Halfdan, while the Queen took her own life in the temple of the Dis.

Heithrek was now accepted as King throughout the realm. He made love to Sifka the daughter of Humli, a prince from the land of the Huns. Their son was called Hlöth. He was brought up with his mother's father.

VIII. King Heithrek went out raiding and marched against the land of the Saxons with a great host. The King of the Saxons sent men to meet him and they made peace with one another, and the King invited Heithrek to a banquet. Heithrek accepted the invitation. The result of this banquet was that Heithrek sought the hand of the King's daughter and married her, receiving much property and land as her dowry; and with that King Heithrek went home to his kingdom. She often used to ask to go to visit her father, and Heithrek was indulgent to her in this matter. Her stepson Angantyr used to go with her.

On one occasion when Heithrek was returning

from a raid, he lay in hiding off the land of the
Saxons. He landed during the night and entered the
building in which his wife was sleeping. He had
only one companion with him. All the sentries were
asleep. He found a handsome man asleep beside his
wife. He took his son Angantyr and carried him
away with him, and returned to his ship, having
first cut off a lock of the man's hair.

Next morning he lay to in the King's berth, and
all the people went to greet him; and a feast was
prepared in his honour. A little later he had a meeting
called and asked if anything was known of his son.
The Queen alleged that he had died suddenly. He
asked her to guide him to his tomb, and when she
said that that would only increase his grief, he replied
that he did not mind that. A search was made
accordingly, and a dog was found wrapped in a
shroud. Heithrek remarked that his son had not
changed for the better. Then the King caused the
man whom he had found asleep to be brought
forward, and he proved to be a bondman. Thereupon Heithrek put away his wife, and then went
home to his kingdom.

One summer as Heithrek was away raiding, he
went into the land of the Huns and harried there,
and Humli his father-in-law fled before him. Heithrek there captured great booty and also Sifka, the
daughter of King Humli, and then returned home
to his kingdom. Their son was called Hlöth, as we
said before. He sent her home shortly after. He also
captured another woman called Sifka from Finland.
She was the loveliest woman ever seen.

One summer he sent men east to Holmgarth to

offer to bring up the child of King Hrollaug, the most powerful king of the time. This he did because he was anxious to act exactly contrary to the whole of his father's advice. Messengers came to Holmgarth and told their errand to the King, who had a young son called Horlaug.

The King replied: "Is it likely that I shall send him my son to bring up, when he has betrayed King Harold his father-in-law and his other relatives and friends?"

But the Queen urged: "Do not be so hasty in refusing this, for if you do not accept his offer the result will certainly be war. I expect it will fare with you as with many another, and war with him will be no trifle. Moreover he has a sword which nothing can withstand, and the man who wields it will always be victorious."

So the King resolved to send his son to Heithrek; and Heithrek was pleased with him and brought him up and loved him much.

Heithrek's father had also counselled him not to tell secrets to his sweetheart.

IX. Every summer King Heithrek went raiding; he always went into the Baltic where he had King Hrollaug's friendly country at hand. On one occasion King Hrollaug invited him to a feast, and Heithrek consulted his friends as to whether he should accept the invitation. They all tried to dissuade him, bidding him bear in mind his father's maxims.

"All his maxims will I disregard," he replied, and sent word to the King that he would be present at the feast.

He divided his host into three parts. One he ordered to guard the ships, the second accompanied him, while the third he ordered to go on shore and conceal themselves in a wood near the house in which the feast was to be held, and to be on the look out in case he should need help. Heithrek went to the feast, and the next day, when the Kings were seated, Heithrek asked where the King's son, his foster-child, was. A search was made for him, but he could not be found. Heithrek was greatly distressed and retired to bed early; and when Sifka joined him she asked why he was distressed.

"That is a difficult matter to talk about," replied he, "because my life is at stake if it becomes known."

She promised to keep the secret, adding:

"Tell me for the sake of the love that is between us."

So Heithrek began:

"As I was riding to the forest yesterday looking for sport, I caught sight of a wild boar and made a thrust at him with my spear; but I missed my aim and the shaft snapped. Then I leapt down from my horse and drew Tyrfing, which was effective as usual, and I slew the boar. But when I looked round there was no-one by except the King's son. But it is a peculiarity of Tyrfing that it must be sheathed with human blood still warm upon it, so I slew the lad. Now this will be the end of me if King Hrollaug hears of it, because we have only a small force here."

Next morning when Sifka came to the Queen, the Queen asked her why Heithrek had been depressed. She said that she did not dare to tell. But the Queen persuaded her to change her mind, so she told the Queen all that Heithrek had told her.

"These are terrible tidings," cried the Queen, and went off in deep grief and told the King; but she added:

"Yet Heithrek has done this against his will."

"Your advice has turned out as I expected," said the King as he left the hall to give orders to his men to arm.

Heithrek had a shrewd notion as to what Sifka had said, and ordered his men to arm themselves secretly, and then to go out in small detachments and try to find out what was happening.

A little later King Hrollaug came in and asked Heithrek to come and have a private talk with him. And when they entered a garden, some men sprang at Heithrek and seized him and cast him into fetters and bound him securely; and he recognised the two men who bound him most tightly as the men whose lives he had saved. The King ordered him to be taken to the forest and hanged. There were two hundred and forty of them all told, and when they entered the forest, King Heithrek's men sprang out at them with his weapons and standard and a trumpet which they blew as they attacked their foes. Their companions concealed in the woods heard the noise and came out to meet King Heithrek's men. And when the natives saw that, they all took to their heels; but most of them were slain. The Goths took their King and released him. Heithrek went to his ships after that, taking with him the King's son whom he had left with the men concealed in the wood.

King Hrollaug now summoned a very large force,

and King Heithrek raided in his kingdom wherever he went.

Then said King Hrollaug to the Queen:

"Your advice has turned out badly for me. I find that our son is with Heithrek, and in his present state of anger he will think nothing of making an end of him in his criminal way, just as he slew his own innocent brother."

"We have been far too easily convinced," replied the Queen. "You saw how popular he was, when no-one would fetter him except two bad men; and our son is taken good care of. This has been a trick of his to make trial of you, and you offered him a poor return for bringing up your child. Send men to him now, and offer to make it up with him, and to give him so much of your territories as you may agree upon with him; and offer him your daughter too, if we can recover our son. That will be better than that you should part from him in enmity. And even if he already has wide territory, he has not a wife as beautiful as she."

"I had not intended to offer her to anyone," replied the King; "but as you are so wise, you shall decide."

Messengers were sent accordingly to King Heithrek to bring about a reconciliation. A council was held and a reconciliation effected by Heithrek's marrying Hergerth, the daughter of King Hrollaug; and she brought him as her dowry Wendland, the province which lies nearest to Reithgotaland.

On one occasion the King was riding his best horse as he was conducting Sifka home. It was late in the evening, and when the King came to a river his horse fell dead. Shortly afterwards, when Sifka attempted to embrace him, he threw her down and broke her leg. Afterwards King Heithrek settled down in his own kingdom and became a great sage.

X. They had a daughter called Hervör who was brought up by a man called Ormar. She was a most beautiful girl, but as tall and strong as a man, and trained herself in the use of bow and arrows.

There was a great man in Reithgotaland called Gestumblindi, who was not on good terms with King Heithrek.

In the King's retinue there were seven men whose duty it was to decide all the disputes that arose in that country.

King Heithrek worshipped Frey, and he used to give Frey the biggest boar he could find. They regarded it as so sacred that in all important cases they used to take the oath on its bristles. It was the custom to sacrifice this boar at the 'sacrifice of the herd.' On Yule Eve the 'boar of the herd' was led into the hall before the King. Then men laid their hands on his bristles and made solemn vows. King Heithrek himself made a vow that however deeply a man should have wronged him, if he came into his power he should not be deprived of the chance of receiving a trial by the King's judges; but he should get off scot free if he could propound riddles which the King could not answer. But when people tried to ask the King riddles, not one was put to him which he could not solve.

The King sent a message to Gestumblindi bidding him come to him on an appointed day; otherwise the King said that he would send to fetch him. Neither alternative pleased Gestumblindi, because he knew himself to be no match for the King in a contest of words; neither did he think he had much to hope from a trial before the judges, for his offences were many. On the other hand, he knew that if the King had to send men to bring him it would cost him his life. Then he proceeded to sacrifice to Othin and to ask his help, promising him great offerings.

One evening a stranger visited Gestumblindi, and said that he also was called Gestumblindi. They were so much alike that neither could be distinguished from the other. They exchanged clothes, and the landowner went into hiding, and everyone thought the stranger was the landowner himself.

This man went to visit the King and greeted him. The King looked at him and was silent.

Gestumblindi said: "I am come, Sire, to make my peace with you."

"Will you stand trial by the judges?" asked the King.

"Are there no other means of escape?" asked Gestumblindi.

"If," replied the King, "you can ask me riddles which I cannot answer, you shall go free."

"I am not likely to be able to do that," replied Gestumblindi; "yet the alternative is severe."

"Do you prefer the trial?" asked the King.

"Nay," said he, "I would rather ask riddles."

"That is quite in order," said the King, "and much depends on the issue. If you can get the better of me you shall marry my daughter and none shall gainsay you. Yet I don't imagine you are very clever, and it has never yet happened that I have

been unable to solve the riddles that have been put
to me."

Then a chair was placed for Gestumblindi, and
the people began to listen eagerly to the words of
wisdom.

Gestumblindi began as follows:

XI. I would that I had that which I had yesterday. Guess
O King, what that was:—Exhauster of men, retarder of
words, yet originator of speech. King Heithrek, read me this
riddle!

Heithrek replied:

Your riddle is a good one, Gestumblindi. I have guessed it.
—Give him some ale. That is what confounds many people's
reason. Some are made garrulous by it, but some become
confused in their speech.

Gestumblindi said:

I went from home, I made my way from home, I looked
upon a road of roads. A road was beneath me, a road above
and a road on every side. King Heithrek, read me this
riddle!

Heithrek replied:

Your riddle is a good one, Gestumblindi. I have guessed it.
You went over a bridge, and the course of the river was
beneath it, and birds were flying over your head and on either
side of you; that was their road; you saw a salmon in the
river, and that was his road.

Gestumblindi said:

What was the drink that I had yesterday? It was neither
wine nor water, mead nor ale, nor any kind of food; and yet
I went away with my thirst quenched. King Heithrek, read
me this riddle!

Heithrek replied:

Your riddle is a good one, Gestumblindi. I have guessed it. You lay in the shade and cooled your lips in dew. But if you are the Gestumblindi I took you for, you are a more intelligent man than I expected; for I had heard that your conversation showed no brains, yet now you are setting to work cleverly.

Gestumblindi said:

I expect that I shall soon come to grief; yet I should like you to listen a while longer.

Then he continued:

Who is that clanging one who traverses hard paths which he has trod before? He kisses very rapidly, has two mouths and walks on gold alone. King Heithrek, read me this riddle!

Heithrek replied:

Your riddle is a good one, Gestumblindi. I have guessed it. That is the goldsmith's hammer, with which gold is forged.

Gestumblindi said:

What is that huge one that passes over the earth, swallowing lakes and pools? He fears the wind, but he fears not man, and carries on hostilities against the sun. King Heithrek, read me this riddle!

Heithrek replied:

Your riddle is a good one, Gestumblindi. I have guessed it. That is fog. One cannot see the sea because of it. Yet as soon as the wind blows, the fog lifts; but men can do nothing to it. Fog kills the sunshine. You have a cunning way of asking riddles and conundrums, whoever you are.

Gestumblindi said:

What is that huge one that controls many things and of which half faces towards Hell? It saves people's lives and grapples with the earth, if it has a trusty friend. King Heithrek, read me this riddle!

Heithrek replied:

Your riddle is a good one, Gestumblindi. I have guessed it.
That is an anchor with its thick strong cable. It controls
many a ship, and grips the earth with one of its flukes which
is pointing towards Hell. It is a means of safety to many
people. Greatly do I marvel at your readiness of speech and
wisdom.

Gestumblindi said:

Ah, but I am now almost at the end of my riddles; yet
everyone is eager to save his life.—What lives in high
mountains? What falls in deep valleys? What lives without
breathing? What is never silent? King Heithrek, read me
this riddle!

Heithrek replied:

Your riddle is a good one, Gestumblindi. I have guessed it.
A raven always lives in high mountains, and dew falls in
deep valleys, a fish lives without breathing, and the booming
waterfall is never silent.

Things are now becoming serious, said Gestumblindi, and
I do not know what is going to happen.—What is the marvel
which I have seen outside Delling's doorway? It points its
head towards Hell and turns its feet to the sun. King Heithrek,
read me this riddle!

Heithrek replied:

Your riddle is a good one, Gestumblindi. I have guessed it.
That is a leek. Its head grows down into the ground, and its
blades upward into the air.

Gestumblindi said:

What is the marvel which I have seen outside Delling's
doorway?—Two restless, lifeless things boiling a wound-
leek. King Heithrek, read me this riddle!

Heithrek replied:

Your riddle is a good one, Gestumblindi. I have guessed it.
That is the smith's bellows which have breath, yet not life.

Gestumblindi said:

What is the marvel which I have seen outside Delling's doorway?—White fliers smiting the rock, and black fliers burying themselves in sand! King Heithrek, read me this riddle!

Heithrek replied:

Your riddle is a good one, Gestumblindi. I have guessed it. But now your riddles are growing trivial. That is hail and rain; for hail beats upon the street; whereas rain-drops fall into the sand and sink into the earth.

Gestumblindi said:

What is the marvel which I have seen outside Delling's doorway? I saw a black hog wallowing in mud, yet no bristles were standing up on his back. King Heithrek, read me this riddle!

Heithrek replied:

Your riddle is a good one, Gestumblindi. I have guessed it. That is a dung-beetle. But we have talked too long when dung-beetles come to exercise the wits of great men.

Gestumblindi said:

"It is best to put off misfortune"; and though there are some who overlook this truth, many will want to go on trying. I myself too see now that I shall have to look out for every possible way of escape. What is the marvel that I have seen outside Delling's doorway? This creature has ten tongues, twenty eyes, forty feet, and walks with difficulty. King Heithrek, read me this riddle!

Heithrek replied:

Your riddle is a good one, Gestumblindi. I have guessed it. That was a sow with nine little pigs.

Then the King had the sow killed and they found they had killed with her nine little pigs, as Gestumblindi had said.

Then the King said:

I am beginning to suspect that I have to deal with a cleverer man than myself in this business; but I don't know who you can be.

Gestumblindi said:

I am such as you can see; and I am very anxious to save my life and be quit of this task.

You must go on asking riddles, replied the King, till you have exhausted your stock, or else till I fail to solve them.

Gestumblindi said:

What is the marvel which I have seen outside Delling's doorway? It flies high, with a whistling sound like the whirring of an eagle. Hard it is to clutch, O King. King Heithrek, read me this riddle!

Heithrek replied:

Your riddle is a good one, Gestumblindi. I have guessed it. That is an arrow, said the King.

Gestumblindi said:

What is the marvel which I have seen outside Delling's doorway? It has eight feet and four eyes, and carries its knees higher than its body. King Heithrek, read me this riddle!

Heithrek replied:

I notice firstly that you have a long hood; and secondly that you look downwards more than most people, since you observe every creature of the earth.—That is a spider.

Gestumblindi said:

What is the marvel which I have seen outside Delling's doorway? It shines upon men in every land; and yet wolves are always struggling for it. King Heithrek, read me this riddle!

Heithrek replied:

Your riddle is a good one, Gestumblindi. I have guessed it.
It is the sun. It gives light to every land and shines down on
all men. But the wolves are called Skalli and Hatti. Those
are the wolves who accompany the sun, one in front and one
behind.

Gestumblindi said:

What is the marvel which I have seen outside Delling's
doorway? It was harder than horn, blacker than the raven,
whiter than the membrane of an egg, straighter than a shaft.
King Heithrek, read me this riddle!

Heithrek replied:

Your riddle is a good one, Gestumblindi. I have guessed it.
You saw an agate, and a sunbeam penetrated the house and
shone upon it. But since you seem to be a learned man, can
you not propound your riddles without always beginning
them in the same way?

Then said Gestumblindi:

Two bond-women, fair-haired brides, were carrying ale
to the store-room. The cask was not turned by hands, nor
clinched by hammers; and he who made it strutted about
outside the islands. King Heithrek, read me this riddle!

Heithrek replied:

Your riddle is a good one, Gestumblindi. I have guessed it.
These are eider duck laying their eggs. The eggs are not
made with hammer or hands, and the hand-maidens put the
ale into the egg-shell.

Gestumblindi said:

He who has got but a little sword and is very short of
learning has to look out for help. I would like to talk still
further.—Who are those ladies of the lofty mountain? A
woman begets by a woman; a maid has a son by a maid; and
these good-wives have no husbands. King Heithrek, read me
this riddle!

Heithrek replied:

Your riddle is a good one, Gestumblindi. I have guessed it. They are two Angelicas joined together, and a young angelica shoot is growing between them.

Gestumblindi said:

Who are the girls who fight without weapons around their lord? The dark red ones always protect him, and the fair ones seek to destroy him. King Heithrek, read me this riddle!

Heithrek replied:

Your riddle is a good one, Gestumblindi. I have guessed it. That is a game of chess. The pieces smite one another without weapons around the king, and the red assist him.

Gestumblindi said:

Who are the merry-maids who glide over the land for their father's pleasure? They bear a white shield in winter and a black one in summer. King Heithrek, read me this riddle!

Heithrek replied:

Your riddle is a good one, Gestumblindi. I have guessed it. Those are ptarmigan.

Gestumblindi said:

Who are the damsels who go sorrowing for their father's pleasure? These white-hooded ladies have shining hair, and are very wide awake in a gale. King Heithrek, read me this riddle!

Heithrek replied:

Your riddle is a good one, Gestumblindi. I have guessed it. Those are the billows, which are called Ægir's maidens.

Gestumblindi said:

Who are the maidens who go about many together for their father's pleasure? They have brought trouble to many; and these good-wives have no husbands. King Heithrek, read me this riddle!

Heithrek replied:

Your riddle is a good one, Gestumblindi. I have guessed it. Those are billows like the last.

Gestumblindi said:

Who are the brides who go about the reefs and trail along the firths? These white-hooded ladies have a hard bed and do not play much when the weather is calm. King Heithrek, read me this riddle.

Heithrek replied:

Your riddle is a good one, Gestumblindi. I have guessed it. Those again are Ægir's maidens; but your pleading has now become so weak that you will have to stand trial by the judges.

Gestumblindi said:

I am loath to do so; and yet I fear that it will very soon come to that. I saw a barrow-dweller pass by, a corpse sitting on a corpse, the blind riding on the blind towards the ocean-path. Lifeless was the steed. King Heithrek, read me this riddle!

Heithrek replied:

Your riddle is a good one, Gestumblindi. I have guessed it. It is that you came to a river; and an ice-floe was floating along the stream, and on it a dead horse was lying, and on the horse was a dead snake; and thus the blind was carrying the blind when they were all three together.

Gestumblindi said:

What is that beast which slays people's flocks and is girt around with iron? It has eight horns, yet no head, and it runs when it can. King Heithrek, read me this riddle!

Heithrek replied:

Your riddle is a good one, Gestumblindi. I have guessed it. That is the *Hunn* in chess. It has the same name as a bear. It runs as soon as it is thrown.

Gestumblindi said:

What is that beast which protects the Danes? Its back is bloody, but it shields men, encounters spears and saves men's lives. Man fits his hand to its body. King Heithrek, read me this riddle!

Heithrek replied:

Your riddle is a good one, Gestumblindi. I have guessed it. That is a shield. It protects many people and often has a bloody back.

Gestumblindi said:

A 'nose-goose' (i.e. duck) in former days had grown very big when eager for young. She gathered together her building timber: 'biters of straw' sheltered her, and 'drink's echoing cavern' was above her. King Heithrek, read me this riddle!

Heithrek replied:

Your riddle is a good one, Gestumblindi. I have guessed it. There a duck was sitting on her eggs between the jaws of an ox, which you call 'biters of straw.' The 'echoing cavern' is the skull, and the 'building timber,' the nest.

Gestumblindi said:

Four walking, four hanging, two pointing the way, two warding off the dogs, one, generally dirty, dangling behind! King Heithrek, read me this riddle!

Heithrek replied:

Your riddle is a good one, Gestumblindi. I have guessed it. That is a cow. She has four feet and four udders, two horns and two eyes, and the tail dangles behind.

Gestumblindi said:

Who is that solitary one who sleeps in the grey ash, and is made from stone only? This greedy one has neither father nor mother. There will he spend his life. King Heithrek, read me this riddle.

Heithrek replied:

Your riddle is a good one, Gestumblindi. I have guessed it. That is a spark struck by a flint and hidden in the hearth.

Gestumblindi said:

I saw a horse standing...

Then the King said:

My retinue shall read this riddle.

They made many guesses, but not particularly good ones. And when the King saw that they could do nothing he said:

What you call a 'horse' is a piece of linen, and his 'mare' is the weaver's rod; and the linen is shaken up and down.

Gestumblindi said:

Who are the thanes who ride to the meeting, sixteen of them together? They send their men far and wide to make homes of their own. King Heithrek, read me this riddle!

Heithrek replied:

Your riddle is a good one, Gestumblindi. I have guessed it. That is 'King Itrek's game.'

Gestumblindi said:

In summer time at sunset I saw the King's body-guard awake and very joyful. The nobles were drinking their ale in silence, but the ale-butts stood screaming. King Heithrek, read me this riddle!

Heithrek replied:

Your riddle is a good one, Gestumblindi. I have guessed it. That is a sow with her litter. When the little pigs are feeding, she squeals and they are silent.—But I can't imagine who you are who can compose such things so deftly out of such unpromising materials!

The King then silently made a sign that the door of the hall was to be closed.

Gestumblindi said:

I saw maidens like dust. Rocks were their beds. They were black and swarthy in the sunshine, but the darker it grew, the fairer they appeared. King Heithrek, read me this riddle!

Heithrek replied:

Your riddle is a good one, Gestumblindi. I have guessed it. They are pale embers on the hearth.

Gestumblindi said:

I sat on a sail, and saw dead men carrying a channel of blood in the bark of a tree. King Heithrek, read me this riddle!

Heithrek replied:

Your riddle is a good one, Gestumblindi. I have guessed it. You sat on a wall, and watched a hawk flying and carrying an eider duck in its claws.

Gestumblindi said:

Who are those two who have ten feet, three eyes and one tail? King Heithrek, read me this riddle!

Heithrek replied:

You are hard up when you have to turn back to things of long ago to bring forward against me. That is Othin riding his horse Sleipnir. It had eight feet and Othin two, and they had three eyes—Sleipnir two and Othin one.

Gestumblindi said:

Tell me lastly, Heithrek, if you are wiser than any other prince, what did Othin whisper in Balder's ear, before he was placed upon the pyre?

The King replied:

I am sure it was something scandalous and cowardly and thoroughly contemptible. You are the only person who knows the words which you spoke, you evil and wretched creature.

Then the King drew Tyrfing, and struck at Gestumblindi; but he changed himself into a falcon and flew out through the window of the hall. And the sword struck the tail of the falcon; and that is why it has had a short tail ever since, according to heathen superstition. But Othin had now become wroth with the King for striking at him; and that night he was slain.

XII. It is said that King Heithrek had some slaves, nine in all, whom he had taken in a freebooting expedition in the West. They came of noble families, and chafed against their captivity. One night, when King Heithrek lay in bed, attended by only a handful of men, the slaves armed themselves and went to the building in which he lay. They first slew the sentries, and then went and broke into the King's chamber, and slew the King and all who were within. They took the sword Tyrfing, and all the treasure that they found there, and carried everything off with them.

For a while, no one knew who had done the deed or how vengeance was to be taken. Then Angantyr the son of King Heithrek had a meeting called, and by that assembly he was proclaimed King over all the territories that King Heithrek had held. And at the same meeting he swore a solemn oath that he would never sit on his father's throne until he had avenged him.

Shortly after the meeting, Angantyr went away by himself and travelled far and wide searching for these men. One evening he was walking down to the sea along a river called Graf. There he saw three men in a fishing-boat, and presently he saw one of the men catch a fish, and heard him call to one of his companions to hand him a bait-knife to cut off the fish's head. The man replied that he could not spare it. Then the first man said:

"Take down the sword from over there by the rudder, and hand it to me."

And he took it and unsheathed it, and cut off the fish's head, and then spoke a verse:

> This pike at the mouth of the river
> Has paid the penalty
> For the slaughter inflicted on Heithrek,
> 'Neath the Mountains of Harvathi.

Angantyr immediately perceived that it was Tyrfing, and went off at once to the wood and waited there till it was dark. And the fishermen rowed to the land, and went to a tent which they had, and lay down and went to sleep. And when it was close on midnight, Angantyr went up to them and pulled down the tent on top of the slaves and slew all nine of them, and carried off the sword Tyrfing as a sign that he had avenged his father. He then went home and had a great funeral feast held to his father's memory on the banks of the Dnieper, at a place called Arheimar. The kings who ruled at that time were as follows: Humli ruled the Huns, Gizur the Gautar, Angantyr the Goths, Valdar the Danes, Kjar the Gauls; Alrek the Bold ruled the English people.

Hlöth the son of King Heithrek was brought up at the court of King Humli, his grandfather. He was a very handsome and valiant man. There was an old saying at that time that a man was "born with weapons or horses." And the explanation is that it referred to the weapons which were being forged at the time when the man was born; also to any sheep, beasts, oxen and horses that were born about the same time. These were all given to high-born men as an honour to them, as is here related about Hlöth the son of Heithrek:

> In the land of the Huns was Hlöth born
>   In a holy forest glade,
> With ring-bedizened helmet,
>   With dagger and keen-edged blade,
> With byrnie and with broadsword,
>   And noble prancing steed.

Then Hlöth learnt of the death of his father, and also that his brother Angantyr had been made King over all the territory which their father had held. Then King Humli and Hlöth resolved that Hlöth should go and request his brother Angantyr to allow him a share of his father's property, and that he should try first by fair words—as is said here:

> Hlöth, the heir of Heithrek,
>   Came riding from the East,
> To where Angantyr was holding
>   King Heithrek's funeral feast.
> He came to his court in Arheimar
>   Where the Gothic people dwell,
> Demanding his share of the heritage left
>   By the King when he journeyed to Hell.

Hlöth now arrived in Arheimar with a great host as it says here:

> He found a warrior hastening
>   Towards the lofty hall;

And unto this late traveller
  Did Hlöth his greeting call:
O man, make haste to enter
  This hall that towers so high!
    Bid Angantyr speed,
    For great is the need
  We hold a colloquy.

The men entered and went up to Angantyr's table
and saluted the King, saying:

Hlöth, thy warlike brother,
  King Heithrek's valiant heir,
Has sent me hither to thee,
  And bidden me declare
That he wishes to hold converse;
  And though he be young indeed,
Yet he looks a mighty champion,
  Seated high upon his steed.

And when the King heard that, he flung down his
knife upon the table and arose from the feast; and
he put on his corslet and took a white shield in one
hand and the sword Tyrfing in the other. Then a
great din arose in the hall, as is said in the poem:

Then a murmur arose from the warriors,
  And all in the hall drew near,
As the warder reported the message of Hlöth:
  —Everyone lent an ear;
And the men all awaited with quivering breath
  The message of Angantyr.

Then Angantyr said: "Hail, brother! You are
welcome! Come in and drink with us, and let us
first drink mead in memory of our father, to the
honour and glory of us all with full ceremony."

Hlöth said: "We are come hither for a different
purpose than to fill our stomachs."

Then Hlöth cried:

> Of all the possessions of Heithrek
>   The half do I now demand;
> —His spear and blade and treasures,
>   His cattle and his land,
> His handmaids and his bondmen,
>   And the children to them born,
> And the murmuring mill that the bondwomen turn
>   As they wearily grind the corn.
>
> And half of the far-famed Myrkvith,
>   And half of the holy grave
> Far off mid the Gothic peoples,—
>   These also will I have.—
> Half of the noble pillar
>   That stands on Danaper's shore;
> And of Heithrek's castles, land and folk,
>   And half of his golden store!

Cried Angantyr:

> The white-shining shield shall be cloven, brother,
>   And spear on spear shall ring;
> And many a helmet be lowered, brother,
>   In battle for this thing,
> Ere I give thee half my heritage,
>   Or half of the sword Tyrfing.

But Angantyr added:

> I will offer thee wealth in plenty,
>   And all thy heart's desire
> In store of costly treasure,
>   And rings of golden fire;
> Twelve hundred squires will I give thee,
>   Twelve hundred prancing steeds;
>   Twelve hundred men
>   To attend on them
>   And arm them for mighty deeds.

> And every man whom I give thee
>   Shall receive a richer store
> Of rings and costly treasures
>   Than ever he had before.—
> To every man a maiden!
>   To every maid a ring!
> I will clasp a necklace round her throat,
>   A necklace fit for a king!
>
> I will case thee all in silver
>   As thou sittest on thy throne;
> And a third of the Gothic peoples
>   Shall be thine to rule alone;
> With gold shalt thou be covered
>   As thou farest through the land.—
>   Thou shalt dazzle the sight
>   As thou walk'st in the light
> Like the flame of a fiery brand.

XIII. Gizur, a liegeman from the Grytingar, King Heithrek's foster-father, was with King Angantyr. He was a very old man at that time. And when he heard King Angantyr's suggestion, he thought that he was offering too much and said:

> King Angantyr is generous,
>   And royal his offering!
> For thy mother was merely a bondmaid
>   Though thou hadst for thy father a King.
> And though thou art only an outcast,
>   Yet a seat of honour was thine,
> When the Prince was dividing his treasure and land,
>   And his portion to each did assign.

Hlöth grew very angry at being called an outcast and the child of a bondwoman, if he accepted his brother's offer; so he departed at once with all his men and returned home to King Humli, his mother's father, in the land of the Huns. And he told Humli that Angantyr his brother had not granted him an equal share. King Humli enquired as to all that had passed between them, and was very angry that Hlöth, the son of his daughter, should be called the son of a bondmaid, and he cried:

> We will stay in our homes for the winter,
>   And as princes are wont when they dine,
> We will hold high converse together,
>   Quaffing the costly wine.
> We will call on the Hunnish people
>   To arm them with spear and with shield.—
>   They shall march to the fight
>   Right royally dight,
>   And conquer their foes in the field.

Then he added:

> We will summon a mighty host, Hlöth,
>   And shield on shield will clang,
> As the warriors arm them from twelve years old,
>   And the wild colts gallop along.
>   And the Huns shall mass
>   Ere the winter pass,
>   And assemble a countless throng.

That winter, King Humli and Hlöth remained quiet, but the following spring they collected such a large army that the land of the Huns was swept bare of fighting men. All those of twelve years old and upwards, who were fit for military service and could carry arms, joined the army, and all the horses of two years old and upwards. The host was now so big that thousands and nothing less than thousands could be counted in the legions. And a commander was set over every 'thousand,' and a standard was set up over every legion. And there were five 'thousand' in each legion, each 'thousand' containing thirteen

'hundreds,' and each 'hundred' four times forty men;
and these legions were thirty three in number.

When these troops had assembled, they rode
through the forest which was called Myrkvith, and
which separated the land of the Huns from that of
the Goths. And when they emerged from the forest,
they came upon a thickly inhabited country with
level fields; and on these plains there was a fine
fortress. It was under the command of Hervör, the
sister of Angantyr and Hlöth, and Ormar, her foster-
father was with her. They had been appointed to
defend the land against the Hunnish host, and they
had a large army there.

XIV. It happened one morning at sunrise that as
Hervör was standing on the summit of a tower over
the gate of the fortress, she looked southwards towards the forest, and saw clouds of dust arising from
a great body of horse, by which the sun was hidden
for a long time. Next she saw a gleam beneath the
dust, as though she were gazing on a mass of gold
—fair shields overlaid with gold, gilded helmets and
white corslets. Then she perceived that it was the
Hunnish host coming on in vast numbers. She
descended hastily and called her trumpeter, and bade
him sound the assembly.

Then said Hervör: "Take your weapons and arm
for battle; and do thou, Ormar, ride against the
Huns and offer them battle before the Southern
Gate."

Ormar replied: "I will certainly take my shield
and ride with the companies of the Goths. I will
challenge the Huns and offer them battle before the
Southern Gate."

Then Ormar rode out of the fortress against the Huns. He called loudly bidding them ride up to the fort, saying:

"Outside the gate of the fortress, in the plains to the south—there will I offer you battle. Let those who arrive first await their foes!"

Then Ormar rode back to the fortress, and found Hervör and all her host armed and ready. They rode forthwith out of the fort with all their host against the Huns, and a great battle began between them. But the Hunnish host was far superior in numbers, so that Hervör's troops began to suffer heavy losses; and in the end Hervör fell, and a great part of her army round about her. And when Ormar saw her fall, he fled with all those who still survived. Ormar rode day and night as fast as he could to King Angantyr in Arheimar. The Huns then proceeded to ravage and burn throughout the land.

And when Ormar came into the presence of King Angantyr, he cried:

> From the south have I journeyed hither
>   To bear these tidings to thee:—
> The whole of the forest of Myrkvith
>   Is burnt up utterly;
> And the land of the Goths is drenched with blood
>   As our warriors fall and die.

Then he continued:

> All of thy noblest warriors
>   On the field are lying dead.
> King Heithrek's daughter fell by the sword;
>   She drooped and bowed her head.
> Thy sister Hervör is now no more.—
>   By the Huns was her life-blood shed.

O prouder and lighter the maiden's step
  As she wielded spear and sword
Than if she were sped to her trysting place,
  Or her seat at the bridal-board!

When King Angantyr heard that, he drew back
his lips, and it was some time before he spoke. Then
he said:
"In no brotherly wise hast thou been treated, my
noble sister!"
Then he surveyed his retinue, and his band of
men was but small; then he cried:

The Gothic warriors were many,
  As they sat and drank the mead;
But now when many are called for,
  The array is poor indeed!
Not a man in the host will adventure—
  Though I offer a rich reward—
    To take his shield,
    And ride to the field,
  To seek out the Hunnish horde.

Then Gizur the Old cried:

I will crave no single farthing,
  Nor ringing coin of gold;
    I will take my shield
    And ride to the field
  To the Huns with their myriads untold.
And the message of war that you send to the host
  Will I carry, and there unfold.

It was a rule with King Heithrek that if his
army was invading a land, and the King of that
land had set up hazel stakes to mark the spot on
which the battle was to take place, then the vikings
should not go raiding till the battle had been fought.

Gizur armed himself with good weapons and leapt on his horse as if he had been a young man. Then he cried to the King:

"Where shall I challenge the host of the Huns to battle?"

King Angantyr replied: "Challenge them to battle at Dylgia and on Dunheith, and upon all the heights of Jösur, where the Goths have often won renown by glorious victories!"

Then Gizur rode away until he came to the host of the Huns. He rode just within earshot, and then called loudly, crying:

> Your host is panic stricken,
>   And your prince is doomed to fall;
> Though your banners are waving high in the air,
>   Yet Othin is wroth with you all.
> Come forth to the Jösur Mountains,
>   On Dylgia and Dunheith come fight;
>   For I make a sure boast,
>   In the heart of your host
> The javelin of Othin will light!

When Hlöth heard Gizur's words, he cried:

"Lay hold upon Gizur of the Grytingar, Angantyr's man, who has come from Arheimar!"

King Humli said: "We must not injure heralds who travel about unattended."

Gizur cried: "You Hunnish dogs are not going to overcome us with guile."

Then Gizur struck spurs into his horse and rode back to King Angantyr, and went up to him and saluted him. The King asked him if he had parleyed with the Huns.

Gizur replied: "I spoke with them and I chal-

lenged them to meet us on the battle-field of Dunheith and in the valleys of Dylgia."

Angantyr asked how big the army of the Huns was.

"Their host is very numerous," replied Gizur.
"There are six legions in all, and five 'thousands' in
every legion, and each 'thousand' contains thirteen
'hundreds,' and in every 'hundred' there are a
hundred and sixty men."

Angantyr asked further questions about the host
of the Huns.

He then sent men in all directions to summon every
man who was willing to support him and could bear
weapons. He then marched to Dunheith with his
army, and it was a very great host. There the host
of the Huns came against him with an army half as
big again as his own.

XV. Next day they began their battle, and they
fought together the whole day, and at evening they
went to their quarters. They continued fighting for
eight days, but the princes were then still all un-
wounded, though none could count the number of
the slain. But both day and night troops came
thronging round Angantyr's banner from all quarters; and so it came about that his army never grew
less.

The battle now became fiercer than ever. The
Huns were desperate, for they now saw that their
only chance of escaping annihilation lay in victory,
and that sorry would be their lot if they had to ask
for quarter from the Goths. The Goths on the other
hand were defending their freedom and their native
land against the Huns; so they stood fast and en-
couraged one another to fight on. Then towards the

close of the day the Goths made so fierce an attack
that the line of the Huns recoiled before it. And when
Angantyr saw that, he pressed forward from behind
the rampart of shields into the forefront of the battle,
and grasping Tyrfing in his hand, mowed down both
men and horses. Then the ranks fell apart in front
of the Kings of the Huns, and Hlöth exchanged
blows with his brother. There fell Hlöth and King
Humli, and then the Huns took to flight. The Goths
cut them down and made such a great slaughter that
the rivers were dammed with the bodies and diverted
from their courses, and the valleys were full of dead
men and horses. Angantyr then went to search
among the slain, and found his brother Hlöth. Then
he cried:

> I offered thee wealth unstinted, brother,
>   And treasures manifold,—
> Riches of cattle and land, brother,
>   Riches of glittering gold;
> But now thou hast wagered and lost in the battle
>   Thy desires and glories untold.
>
> A curse has fallen upon us, brother,
>   I have dealt destruction to thee;
> And ne'er shall the deed be forgotten, brother;
>   Full ill is the norns' decree!

XVI. Angantyr ruled Reithgotaland as King for
a long time. He was powerful and generous and
a great warrior, and lines of kings are sprung from
him.

He had a son called Heithrek Wolfskin who ruled
after him for a long time in Reithgotaland. Heithrek
had a daughter called Hild, who was the mother of
Halfdan the Valiant, the father of Ivar Vithfathmi.

Ivar Vithfathmi went with his army into the Swedish
kingdom, as is told in the Sagas of the Kings. And
King Ingjald the Wicked was panic-stricken at the
approach of his army, and burned the roof over himself and all his retinue at a place called Ræning. Ivar
Vithfathmi then conquered all Sweden. He also subdued Denmark and Courland and the land of the
Saxons and Esthonia, and all the eastern realms as
far as Russia. He also ruled the land of the Saxons
in the West and conquered the part of England
which was called Northumbria.

Then he conquered all Denmark and set over it
King Valdar, to whom he married his daughter
Alfhild. Their sons were Harold Hilditönn and
Randver who afterwards fell in England. And when
Valdar died in Denmark, Randver got possession of
the Danish kingdom and made himself King over it.
And King Harold Hilditönn got himself proclaimed
King of Gautland, and he afterwards conquered all
the kingdoms already mentioned, which King Ivar
Vithfathmi had held.

King Randver married Asa, the daughter of
King Harold of the Red Moustache from Norway.
Their son was Sigurth Hring. King Randver died
suddenly, and Sigurth Hring succeeded to the
Kingdom of Denmark. He fought against King
Harold Hilditönn at the Battle of Bravöll in East
Gautland, and there King Harold fell, and a great
multitude of his army with him. This battle and the
one which Angantyr and his brother Hlöth fought
at Dunheith are the battles which have been most
famous in stories of old. Never were any greater
slaughters made.

King Sigurth Hring ruled the Kingdom of the Danes till the day of his death; and his son Ragnar Lothbrok succeeded him.

Harold Hilditönn had a son called Eystein the Wicked, who succeeded to the Swedish Realm after his father, and ruled it until he was slain by the sons of Ragnar Lothbrok, as is related in the Saga of Ragnar Lothbrok. The sons of Ragnar Lothbrok conquered all the Swedish Kingdom; and after the death of King Ragnar, his son, Björn Ironside, inherited Sweden, and Sigurth Denmark, Hvitserk the Eastern Realm, and Ivar the Boneless England.

The sons of Björn Ironside were Eric and Refil. The latter was a warrior-prince and sea-king. King Eric ruled the Swedish Realm after his father, and lived but a short time. Then Eric the son of Refil succeeded to the Kingdom. He was a great warrior and a very powerful King. The sons of Eric Björnsson were Önund of Upsala and King Björn. Then the Swedish Realm again came to be divided between brothers. They succeeded to the Kingdom on the death of Eric Refilsson. King Björn built a house called 'Barrow,' and he himself was called Björn of the Barrow. Bragi the poet was with him. King Önund had a son called Eric, and he succeeded to the throne at Upsala after his father. He was a mighty King. In his days Harold the Fair-haired made himself King of Norway. He was the first to unite the whole of that country under his sway.

Eric at Upsala had a son called Björn, who came to the throne after his father and ruled for a long time. The sons of Björn, Eric the Victorious, and Olaf succeeded to the kingdom after their father.

Olaf was the father of Styrbjörn the Strong. In their days King Harold the Fair-haired died. Styrbjörn fought against King Eric his father's brother at Fyrisvellir, and there Styrbjörn fell. Then Eric ruled Sweden till the day of his death. He married Sigrith the Ambitious. They had a son called Olaf who was accepted as King in Sweden after King Eric. He was only a child at the time and the Swedes carried him about with them, and for this reason they called him 'Skirt-King,' and then, later, Olaf the Swede. He ruled for a long time and was a powerful King. He was the first king of Sweden to be converted, and in his days, Sweden was nominally Christian.

King Olaf the Swede had a son called Önund who succeeded him. He died in his bed. In his day fell King Olaf the Saint at Stiklestad. Olaf the Swede had another son called Eymund, who came to the throne after his brother. In his day the Swedes neglected the Christian religion, but he was King for only a short time.

There was a great man of noble family in Sweden called Steinkel. His mother's name was Astrith, the daughter of Njal the son of Fin the Squinter, from Halogaland; and his father was Rögnvald the Old. Steinkel was an Earl in Sweden at first, and then after the death of Eymund, the Swedes elected him their King. Then the throne passed out of the line of the ancient kings of Sweden. Steinkel was a mighty prince. He married the daughter of King Eymund. He died in his bed in Sweden about the time that King Harold fell in England.

Steinkel had a son called Ingi, who became King of Sweden after Haakon. Ingi was King of Sweden for a long time, and was popular and a good Christian. He tried to put an end to heathen sacrifices in Sweden and commanded all the people to accept Christianity; yet the Swedes held to their ancient faith. King Ingi married a woman called Mær who had a brother called Svein. King Ingi liked Svein better than any other man, and Svein became thereby the greatest man in Sweden. The Swedes considered that King Ingi was violating the ancient law of the land when he took exception to many things which Steinkel his father had permitted, and at an assembly held between the Swedes and King Ingi, they offered him two alternatives, either to follow the old order, or else to abdicate. Then King Ingi spoke up and said that he would not abandon the true faith; whereupon the Swedes raised a shout and pelted him with stones, and drove him from the assembly.

Svein, the King's brother-in-law, remained behind in the assembly, and offered the Swedes to do sacrifices on their behalf if they would give him the Kingdom. They all agreed to accept Svein's offer, and he was then recognised as King over all Sweden. A horse was then brought to the assembly and hewn in pieces and cut up for eating, and the sacred tree was smeared with blood. Then all the Swedes abandoned Christianity, and sacrifices were started again. They drove King Ingi away; and he went into Vestergötland. Svein the Sacrificer was King of Sweden for three years.

King Ingi set off with his retinue and some of his followers, though it was but a small force. He then rode eastwards by Småland and into Östergötland and then into Sweden. He rode both day and night, and came upon Svein suddenly in the early morning. They caught him in his house and set it on fire and burned the band of men who were within.

There was a baron called Thjof who was burnt inside. He had been previously in the retinue of Svein the Sacrificer. Svein himself left the house, but was slain immediately.

Thus Ingi once more received the Kingdom of Sweden; and he reestablished Christianity and ruled the Kingdom till the end of his life, when he died in his bed.

King Steinkel had, besides Ingi, another son Hallstein who reigned along with his brother. Hallstein's sons were Philip and Ingi, and they succeeded to the Kingdom of Sweden after King Ingi the elder. Philip married Ingigerth, the daughter of King Harold the son of Sigurth. He reigned for only a short time.

APPENDIX TO PART I

THE COMBAT AT SAMSØ AND HJALMAR'S DEATH SONG

The following passage is taken from an early text of the *Saga of Hervör and Heithrek* (MS. 2845 in the Royal Library at Copenhagen) where it occurs immediately after the earl's speech (" The death of mighty men " etc.) on p. 92[1].

When the brothers came home they made ready to go to the combat, and their father accompanied them to the ship and gave the sword Tyrfing to Angantyr, saying:

" I think that you will have need of good weapons now."

He then bade them farewell, and so they parted.

And when the brothers came to Samsø they saw two ships lying in a harbour which was called Munarvag. The ships were of the kind called 'Ash.' The brothers concluded that these must be the ships of Hjalmar and Odd the Far-travelling, who was called Örvar-Odd. The sons of Arngrim then drew their swords and gnawed the rims of their shields and worked themselves up into the berserks' fury. Then they sallied forth, six against each 'Ash,' but so brave were the men whom they encountered on board that they all drew their weapons, and not one fled from his post, and not one spoke a word of fear. And

[1] Printed in Wimmer's *Oldnordisk Læsebog* (4th ed.) p. 29 ff. The poetry is also found, though with many divergent readings, in *Örvar-Odds Saga*, ch. 14 (*Fornaldarsögur*, Vol. II, p. 217 ff.).

the berserks made their way up one side of the ship and down the other and slew them all. Then they landed and began to howl.

Hjalmar and Odd had landed on the Island to find out if the berserks had come. And as they made their way from the forest to join their ships, the berserks were leaving the ships with bloody weapons and drawn swords. But by this time the berserk fury had passed away from them, and at such times their strength is reduced like that of people who are recovering from illness of some kind.

Then said Odd:

> I never knew aught of terror
>   Till today when the berserks came.
> They have sailed to this isle in their ashen ships,
>   All twelve devoid of shame,
> And landed with many a whoop and yell,
>   Those wretches of evil fame.

Then said Hjalmar to Odd: "Do you see that all our men are fallen? It is my belief that we shall all be Othin's guests tonight in Valhalla."

—And it is said that that was the only word of fear ever uttered by Hjalmar.

Odd replied: "My advice would be that we should make off to the wood; for we shall never be able to put up a fight, being only two against twelve—and twelve too who have slain the twelve bravest men in Sweden."

Then said Hjalmar: "We will never flee from our foes. Rather will we suffer the worst that their weapons can inflict. I am going to fight against the berserks."

"Not so," replied Odd; "I have no mind to visit Othin tonight. It is all these berserks who must perish before evening comes; but you and I will be left alive."

An account of their dialogue is found in these verses which Hjalmar chanted:

> Twelve berserks hasten onward,
>   Inglorious warriors;—
> Leaving their warships on they come;
>   And when night's shadow lowers
> We two shall feast in Othin's hall,
>   Leaving them conquerors.

But Odd replied:

> This is the answer I give thee:—
>   In Othin's hall tonight,
>   Twelve berserks shall feast,
>   Every one as a guest,
> While we shall live on in the light.

Hjalmar and Odd saw that Angantyr had Tyrfing in his hand, for it flashed like a sunbeam.

Hjalmar said: "Will you fight against Angantyr alone, or against all his eleven brothers?"

"I will fight against Angantyr," replied Odd; "He will give mighty strokes with Tyrfing; but I have more faith in the protection of my shirt than in that of your mail-coat."

Then cried Hjalmar: "When did you and I ever go to battle and you took the lead of me? You want to fight Angantyr because you hold that to be the deed of greater prowess. I am the leader in this combat, however, and far other was the vow I made to the daughter of the King of the Swedes than to let you or anybody else come before me in the fight. It is I who am going to fight Angantyr.

And with that he drew his sword and stepped forth to meet Angantyr and they commended one another to Valhalla[1]. Hjalmar and Angantyr then made ready for the combat, and mighty strokes fell thick and fast between them.

Odd called to the berserks, saying:

> Man to man should a warrior fight
> Who would win a well-fought day,—
> Unless it be that his courage fail,
> Or his valour has ebbed away.

Then Hjörvarth advanced, and he and Odd had a stiff encounter; but Odd's silken shirt was so strong that no weapon could pierce it. And so good was his sword that it cut through iron as easily as cloth; and few strokes had he dealt ere Hjörvarth fell dead.

Then Hervarth came on and the same thing happened;—then Hrani, then each of the others in turn. And with such force did Odd encounter them all that he slew every one of the eleven brothers. As for the combat between Hjalmar and Angantyr, the upshot was that Hjalmar was wounded in sixteen places, and then Angantyr fell dead.

Then Odd went over to where Hjalmar lay and cried:

> O Hjalmar! Why has thy face grown pale
> As the face of men who die?
> Wide gape the rents in byrnie and helm,
> And I fear that the end draws nigh;
> And the strength of manhood has gone from thine arm,
> And the light of life from thine eye.

[1] In late (paper) MSS. the following passage is here added.— "Angantyr said: 'It is my wish that if any of us escapes from here we should not rob one another of our weapons. If I die, I wish to have Tyrfing in the barrow with me. Odd likewise shall have his shirt and Hjalmar his weapons!' And they agreed that those who were left alive were to raise a barrow for the others."

Then follows a long description of the fighting.

Hjalmar made answer[1]:

With sixteen wounds is my mailcoat rent,
    And the world is fading fast.
Blindly I tread in the gathering gloom,
    Pierced to the heart at the last
By Angantyr's sword with its pitiless point
    And its edges in poison cast.

*I have given no cause to Ingibjörg
    To hold my prowess light;
It shall never be said by our maidens at home
    That I gave one thought to flight.
They shall hear how the battle was fought and won.—
    How I wielded my sword in the fight.

Five manors were mine, all nobly appointed,
    Where I might have tarried and made good cheer.
Yet my heart was stirred by a restless longing
    That urged me onward to Samsø here,
Where, pierced by the sword, with my life blood out pouring,
    I shall linger and die on this island so drear.

In my mind I can see the henchmen
    Drinking mead in my father's hall.—
A circle of gold is round every throat,
    And joy is among them all.
My merry companions are drinking their ale,
    Till thought and care are no more,
While I, torn with wounds from a murderous sword,
    Perish here on this island shore.

*The lofty halls of Sigtun,
    I see them from far away;
And the maidens who sought to withhold us
    As we hastened forth on our way.

[1] This poem is given more fully in *Örvar-Odds Saga* than in *Hervarar Saga*. The strophes which occur only in the former are marked with an asterisk. I have re-arranged the order of the stanzas, in regard to which there is considerable variation between the two texts.

I shall never again see those maidens,
  Or talk with the warriors bold,
Or drink fair ale in the King's high hall,
  As I did in the days of old.

In my heart a voice still lingers,
  The voice of a maiden fair,
Who rode with me forth to Agni's meads,
  And bade farewell to me there.
And true, too true, were the words she spake
  From the depths of her despair,
That never again should I touch her lips,
  Or tangle her golden hair.

In my ear a song is ringing,
  An echo from out the East,—
I heard it from Soti's cliffs on the night
  When I left my friends at the feast.
How could I know that never again
  Should I hear the maidens' lay,
As I hastened forth with my heart aflame,
  And my good ship sailed away?

*In token of what has befallen,
  My helmet and corslet take,
And bear them forth to the King's high hall.—
  'Tis the last request I make.
The prince's daughter, fair Ingibjörg,
  Will be stricken with grief and pain
When she looks on my good shield hacked and rent,
  And knows that her love was vain.

Draw from my arm this token,
  This ring of gleaming gold;
And bear it to Ingibjörg the fair,
  Lest she deem my love grown cold.
Young is the maid to bear the sorrow
  Her heart must then endure,
When I ride not home to greet her,
  When I keep not my tryst as of yore

*I left the youthful Ingibjörg
   Upon that fateful day,
When rashly we placed our fortunes
   In the hands of Destiny.
O heavy will be the maiden's grief,
   The sorrow she must endure
When she knows I have fallen in battle,
   And will enter her hall no more.

From the tree tops away to the Eastward
   There gather a loathly brood:—
Raven and eagle are swooping
   To wet their bills in my blood.
Full many a feast has the eagle had
   Of carrion slain by me:
      I have fought my last fight,
         And I pass to the night;
      And now he shall feast on me.

Then Hjalmar died[1]. Odd brought the tidings
to Sweden; and the King's daughter could not
bear to live after Hjalmar, so she took her own
life. Angantyr and his brothers were laid in a barrow in Samsø with all their weapons.

[1] In paper MSS. the following passage occurs here:

"Odd remained there all night. In the morning he brought
together the bodies of all the berserks and then set about building
barrows. The islanders built chambers of great oaks as Odd directed
them, and then piled up stones and sand on the top. They were
strongly constructed, and it was a great achievement. Odd was busy
at this work for a fortnight. Then he placed the berserks in with
their weapons and closed the barrows. After this Odd took Hjalmar's
body and carried it to a ship and conveyed it to Sweden."

PART II

BALLADS

BALLADS

GENERAL INTRODUCTION

I. The ballads of the Faroe Islands aroused the interest of Ole Worm as early as 1639; but the five ballads which he took down are no longer extant, and we know of them only from a reference by Peder Syv[1] towards the close of the seventeenth century. In 1673 Lucas Debes[2] wrote a description of the islands which contained an account of their dances and songs; but unfortunately he did not transcribe any of the ballads. Indeed the balladry and songs attracted little general attention till the close of the eighteenth century, when Jens Kristjan Svabo devoted himself to a careful study of the language and a collection of the ballads of his native Islands.

In 1781–2, during a visit to the Faroes, Svabo turned his attention especially to Faroese folk-songs and made a MS. collection of fifty-two ballads, which were purchased by the Crown Prince and presented to the Royal Library at Copenhagen. It is interesting to note that Svabo, like his contemporary Bishop Percy[3], thought it necessary to apologise in his preface

[1] Cf. S. Grundtvig, *Meddelelse Angående Færøernes Litteratur og sprog*, in *Aarbøger for Nordisk Oldkyndighed*, published by the Royal Norse Early Text Society (Copenhagen), 1882, p. 358.

[2] *Færoa Reserata* (Copenhagen, 1673), pp. 251 and 308 (tr. John Sterpin, London, 1676).

[3] *Reliques*, Vol. I, *Epistle to the Countess of Northumberland*.

for making the collection, and humbly claims for it an interest merely antiquarian. It is clear, however, from his tone throughout the Preface, that Svabo had a far more scholarly appreciation of the value of his material than had Percy. Indeed it would be difficult to overestimate the debt which all succeeding students of Faroese ballads owe to him. Disappointed in his hopes of public recognition of his work done for the Civil Service, he retired to the Islands, where, in solitude and poverty, he devoted himself, till his death in 1829, to the collection and transcription of ballad material. His personal help and example inspired other Faroe-islanders to make collections for themselves, some of which, notably Klemmentsen's *Sandoyjarbók*, are among our best authorities for the ballads today. His own ballad collection, still in MS. in the Royal Library at Copenhagen, has never been published; but Schrøter, Lyngbye and Hammershaimb all owed their incentive and inspiration to his work. To study the history of Faroese ballad collections without realising the force of Svabo's personality is to leave Hamlet out of the play.

In 1817 the Danish botanist, Hans Kristjan Lyngbye visited the Faroes, where he became acquainted with "the learned Svabo" as he calls him, and also with Johan Henrik Schrøter, a clergyman on Suderø, himself a keenly interested ballad collector, and, incidentally, the first to make a collection of Faroese folk-tales in prose. Partly from these men, and partly from oral recitations and material supplied by Provost Hentze, Lyngbye was able to gather together a considerable body of Faroese ballads which, with the support and encouragement

of Bishop P. E. Müller, he published at Copenhagen in 1822, under the title of *Færöiske Kvæder
om Sigurd Fofnersbane og hans Æt.*

Unfortunately Lyngbye knew no Icelandic and
very little Faroese, and his work necessarily suffers
in consequence. Still more unfortunate was his
unscientific handling of material and lack of literary
conscience, which permitted his cutting out, adding
and transposing stanzas—and again we are reminded of the *Reliques*—till the original form of
a ballad is sometimes entirely lost. Fortunately,
however, most of the material that he had at his
command is still preserved. It is to be noted that
the qualities which go to make an ideal *collector* of
ballads do not always imply an ideal editor of the
material collected. The great collector of Jutland
ballads and folk-lore, Evald Tang Kristensen, has
started a new and sounder tradition by a reverent
in-gathering of all that formed part of the common
stock of peasant lore in his day[1]. The sifting of
material is wisely left to the trained scholar, and, one
hopes, to a later and less intrepid generation[2].

The tradition started by Svabo and Lyngbye was
carried on by V. U. Hammershaimb, himself a
native of the Islands and a great lover of Faroese
folk-lore. During the years 1847–8, and again in
1853, he visited the Faroes expressly to study the
dialects, and to collect the native ballads and folk-
lore, which he published under the title of *Færöiske*

[1] Cf. W. A. Craigie, *Evald Tang Kristensen, A Danish Folk-lorist*,
in *Folklore*, Vol. IX, 1898, pp. 194–220.
[2] Cf. C. J. Sharp, *English Folk Songs from the Southern Appalachians* (London, 1917), p. xxii.

Kvæder in the *Nordiske Literatur-Samfund*, the *Antiquarisk Tidsskrift*, etc.

Like Svabo, Hammershaimb eventually returned and settled on the Faroes; but unfortunately, owing to the pressure of his administrative duties, he was never able to spare time for a final revision of his collection, though urged repeatedly to the work by his friend Svend Grundtvig. Ultimately, however, when Grundtvig himself undertook to make an exhaustive critical edition of the Faroese ballads in all their variant forms, Hammershaimb placed all his material in his hands.

Svend Grundtvig and his colleague J. Bloch, of the Royal Library staff, completed in 1876 their great fifteen vol. MS. collection of Faroese ballads with all their known variants, *Føroyja Kvæði— Corpus Carminum Faeroensium—Færøernes Gamle Folkeviser*. This was afterwards increased by Bloch to sixteen volumes by the addition of much new material, some of which was collected by Jakobsen in his journey to the Faroes in 1887[1]. Before beginning the work Grundtvig had every available version, whether in public or private hands, at his disposal, so that he had a magnificent apparatus criticus. Unfortunately the work has never been published, so that owing to the difficulties of communication with Denmark (which have proved to be insuperable) it has been impossible for me to consult it. The first three volumes, however, which include all the Faroese ballads translated below, are based on Hammershaimb's collections of 1851–1855. Ham-

---

[1] Axel Olrik, *Om Svend Grundtvigs og Jörgen Blochs Føroyjakvæði og færøske ordbog*, in *Arkiv för Nordisk Filologi* (Lund, 1890), p. 249.

mershaimb was himself a genuine scholar with a sensitive literary conscience and a thorough knowledge of all the Faroese dialects, and his work is spoken of in the highest terms by Grundtvig in his article on the *Corpus Carminum Faroensium*[1]. Moreover Hammershaimb had consulted all the other available versions of these ballads before printing; so that it is improbable that when a comparison of the texts can be made much alteration will be required.

II. The Faroe Islands are probably the only place to be found in Western Europe where ballads are still sung to the accompaniment of the dance. The dance and song, it must be confessed, are gradually losing their original character, while the ballads are often long and unwieldy, sometimes, as in the Ballad of Ívint Herintsson, running to five divisions (*Tættir*) and over three hundred and fifty verses. The verses are frequently chanted in a solemn recitative, while the ballad tunes tend to be confined chiefly to the refrains. The method of supplying the melody, however, is subject to almost endless variation. Sometimes old native folk tunes are attached to special ballads, e.g. in the case of *Vi hugged mid kaarde*; sometimes native ballads are sung to Danish folk melodies and refrains as, e.g. *Grindevisen*, sung to the tune of the Danish *Burmand holder i Fjældet ut*. Sometimes in the Faroese repertoire, Norse ballads are found complete with their own melodies, e.g. *Sømandsviserne*, or sung to Danish folk-tunes, e.g. *Zinklars Vise*. Most curious of all is the method not infrequently resorted to in

---

[1] Sv. Grundtvig, *Færøernes Litteratur og Sprog*, in *Aarbøg for Nord. Oldk.*, 1882, p. 364.

modern times of singing native ballads, often of
modern origin, to the tunes of the Protestant
Psalmody—a custom which may have had its origin
in the common practice of singing both ballads and
psalms on all momentous occasions, such as on the
night of a wedding, or before starting on a big fishing
expedition. The Islanders have little idea of tone
or melody and do not sing well; and eye-witnesses
of some of the ballad dances at Thorshaven aver that
the tunes sound less like dance music than melan-
choly dirges. In *Folkesangen paa Færøerne (Færøske
Kvadmelodier)*, pp. 85–140, Thuren has published a
large number of original ballad tunes. The characteristic motifs of folk tunes are traceable throughout, as well as their elusive qualities. Thus we find,
side by side with airs based on the ordinary major
and minor scales, others which, like mediaeval
church music, are based on a 'modal' or 'gapped'
tonal system. Indeed traces of the pentatonic scale
are not infrequently met with, especially in the tunes
attached to the earlier ballads. The majority of
Faroese melodies, however, have only one gap and
have more in common with the system of notation
found in Gregorian music than with the pentatonic
scale of many Hebridean lays. A further characteristic of folk music which appears in most Faroese airs
is the curious form of close which rarely occurs on the
tonic. Not infrequently the theme ends on the leading
note or supertonic which strikes the ear with a perpetual surprise, the cadence leading one to anticipate
a repetition rather than a conclusion of the air. The
reason is that these tunes, like many folk songs from
Somerset, the Appalachians and the Hebrides, were

'circular,' that is, formed for continuous repetition to suit the lengthy nature of the songs and ballads.

The ballad however is not a mere historical relic on the Faroes, but a living literary form. The simplicity of the life, and the absence of class distinction[1], still constitute an atmosphere in some respects not unlike that of Mediaeval Denmark, and the ballad is the favourite form of artistic expression. A whale-hunt, a shipwreck, or the adventures of fishermen in the far north are still made the subject of a new ballad, composed by one or more of the community; and if the result finds general favour it is added to the ballad repertoire along with the ballads of Sir Tristram or Childe Sigurth[2].

In his description of his travels on the Faroes 1847–8, V. U. Hammershaimb[3] says that he took down the greater number of his ballads at Sumbø on Suderø, the most southerly village in the Islands. He describes the ballad dance as follows:

It is the custom here that the same ballad should not be sung more than once a year[4] in the 'dancing-chamber,' so

[1] Cf. N. Annandale, *The Faroes and Iceland* (Oxford, 1905), p. 42.

[2] For interesting accounts of the composition of new ballads, cf. Lyngbye's article in the *Skandinavske Litteraturselskabs Skrifter*, 12th and 13th Annual, p. 234 ff.; also P. E. Müller, Introduction to Lyngbye's *Fær. Kv.*, pp. 14, 15. The *Trawlaravisur* and other ballads, besides the dances and tunes of the Faroe Islands of today, have been investigated by Thuren who published several studies on this most interesting subject, e.g. *Dans og Kvaddigtning paa Færøerne, med et Musikbilag*, 1901. *Folkesangen paa Færøerne*, 1908, etc., (cf. especially *Nyere Danseviser*, pp. 273–282), etc.

[3] *Antiq. Tidsk.*, 1846–1848, pp. 258–267.

[4] According to H. Thuren, *Dansen paa Færøerne* (Copenhagen, 1908), p. 9, a certain fixed number of songs are now sung on Suderø; a great many have been quite forgotten since Hammershaimb wrote.

that the repertoire is obviously extensive, seeing that they
dance at wedding feasts, generally for three days and nights
without cessation. In the special dancing season from Yule
till Lent, the ballads are danced not only on Sundays but
also on the so-called 'Feast Days.' (They do not dance again
from the beginning of Lent till the day after Christmas.)
The dance at Sumbø has characteristics of its own which
differ from those of the rest of the Faroes. The people here
generally sing well and know how to put expression into the
actual dance. Elsewhere on the Islands this is now for the
most part reduced to a uniform stamp with the feet, marking
the melody of the ballad. Moreover they still continue here
in common use both the 'Walking Verse' (*stígingar stev*)
and the more rapid measure 'Tripping Verse' (*trókingar
stev*) of the Round Dance, in which, as a rule, the dancers
hold one another by the hand, forming a circle, dancing
backwards while the verse (*örindi*) is sung, and reversing the
movement with considerable energy during the singing of
the refrain (*viðgangur, niðurlág, stev*). This round dance is
characteristic of Sumbø[1].

For the most part the dance is now performed with
the same speed in both verse and refrain[2], and
though little changed since Hammershaimb wrote,
it tends more and more to become a solemn and
joyless function; and there is a curious unanimity
today among eyewitnesses as to the depressing effect it
has on them. Hjalmar Thuren, writing in later times
(1908), furnishes some additional information as to the
manner of the ballad dance[3]. The ballads are danced
with special zest on the 29th of July, the day of the
anniversary of the death of Saint Olaf, when all the
islanders who can leave their homes flock to Thors-

[1] It is also occasionally danced in Andefjord, but only very rarely
nowadays (cf. H. Thuren, *Dansen paa Færøerne*, p. 8).
[2] *Ib.*, p. 8.   [3] *Ib.*, pp 4–10.

haven and dance from sunset till sunrise. Sometimes the ballads are danced in the open air, and it has been the custom in certain districts from ancient times to hold assemblies for dancing out in the fields on certain fixed days. On the 12th Sunday after Trinity people meet in definite places on the Northern Islands. On the other hand the dance is often the spontaneous outcome of the desire of the moment, "as much to keep themselves warm as for the sake of entertainment." Thus after a whale-hunt the men sometimes dance in their wet, bloody clothes, singing the popular ballad of the ca'ing whale with the refrain:

> To us bold men great joy it is
> To slay a whale!

The dance is always accompanied by song, but instrumental music has never been in use on the Faroes. The time and character of the dance are indicated at the beginning of the ballad by the precentor. This post of honour was originally much sought after and some precentors were famous over the islands for their special rendering of certain ballads, some of which were family possessions in the old days.

When a ballad is concluded, one of those who are taking part straightway begins on a new one, the dance frequently continuing uninterrupted, even when the song is ended. The precentor must have a strong voice and great powers of endurance as the ballads are often very long. He is generally of a lively disposition with some dramatic power, so that by imitating his gesticulations the dancers give character and individuality to the ballad. Thus in the refrain to the *Death-Song of Ragnar Loðbrók*:

> *We struck with the sword*

the dancers stamp on the floor and clap hands together; but they are solemn and silent during the
singing of a sorrowful ballad such as

Queen Dagmar lies sick, etc.

With the ballad dances of the Faroes it is interesting
to compare the ballad dances of the Ukraine and
also the choral dances of a community so far removed
as the Torres Straits. Of these latter Dr Haddon
writes[1]:

The dancing-ground was an oblong space....The drummer
with the singers generally struck up a song, but sometimes
the dancers sang a refrain or called for a song by name. Each
song seemed to be associated with its own particular dance
and to be *accompanied by some story or incident* which was
illustrated by the movements of the dancers.

A much closer parallel, however, is furnished by
the Хороводъ or choral dance of Little Russia.
The Хороводъ, according to the account of an
eye witness[2], is not only a song sung to the accompaniment of a dance; but the song is narrative in form
and answers in all respects to the ballad of North
Western Europe. The dancers join hands and dance
in a circle from west to east, in a contrary direction
to the sun's movements—*withershins* as the Scots
peasants have it. Then, because it is considered
unlucky to do anything *withershins*, in the refrain
the motion is reversed and the dancers pass from
east to west, to counteract the baleful effects of the

[1] *Dances and Dance Paraphernalia*, in *Expedition to the Torres
Straits* (Cambridge, 1904), Vol. IV, p. 292.
[2] Miss Aline Brylinska, who has kindly supplied me with this
information.

first direction. Here too, however, it is interesting to note, the dance is sometimes stationary.

III. Into the rise of the ballads on the Faroes and their exact relation of form and content to the Icelandic *Fornkvæði*[1], and to the *Viser* of Norway[2], Sweden[3], and above all of Denmark[4], it is impossible to enter here. Perhaps the relationship between the ballads of the various countries of the North will never be fully understood. The ramifications are too many and too complex, while too many links in the chain have already been lost in the "scrubby paper books" such as that with which Bishop Percy found the housemaid lighting the parlour fire. And those who would too hastily dogmatise on the 'conveyance,' translation, and borrowing of the various versions receive a wholesome warning from Dr Axel Olrik's analysis[5] of the ancestry and parallel versions of the Scots, Icelandic, Swedish, Norwegian and Danish forms of the ballads of Earl Brand (Dan. *Riboldsvisen*). Moreover it is no easier to generalise about the sources of the Faroese ballad material than about the Danish. The motif of the Faroese *Tristrams Táttur*, also found in the Icelandic ballad of *Tristram*, comes ultimately (through the Tristram's Saga one would suppose) from a French romance; that of

[1] S. Grundtvig and Jón Sigurðsson, *Islenzk Fornkvæði*, in *Nordiske Oldskrifter* (Copenhagen, 1854–85).

[2] Landstad, *Norske Folkeviser* (Christiania, 1853); S. Bugge, 1858.

[3] Geijer and Afzelius, 1814–1816, 1880; Arwidsson, 1834–1842.

[4] S. Grundtvig, *Danmarks Gamle Folkeviser*, 1853–1890. S. Grundtvig and A. Olrik, *Danske Ridderviser*, 1895–1919.

[5] *Riboldsvisen* (a review of von der Recke's *Nogle Folkeviseredaktioner*) in *Danske Studier*, 1906, p. 175 ff.

Nornagest, changed though it is in form, is surely founded on the Icelandic Saga; *Olufu Kvæði* comes no doubt from a Spanish story; and the motif of the Scots ballad of *Binnorie* is "found also among the people of Ireland, Norway, Sweden, Denmark and the Faroes[1]."

It would be pleasant to develop a theory that the purveyors of ballad material were the sailors and merchants who plied up and down the great trade routes in the fourteenth and fifteenth centuries, or even earlier. It has been suggested by Professor Ker[2] and others that Shetland *may* have been "the chief meeting-place or trading station between the ballads of Scotland and Norway." The Shetland ballad of *Sir Orfeo* actually has a refrain in Norn, the Norse dialect spoken in Shetland and the small neighbouring islands till the eighteenth century; while the ballad of *Hildina* taken down by Low[3] on the Island of Foula off Shetland (cf. p. 217 below) is entirely composed in Norn. Indeed we know from Low's account[4] that many ballads and songs must have perished with the language:

Nothing remains but a few names of things and two or three remnants of songs which one old man can repeat;

and further on he continues:

Most of the fragments they have are *old historical ballads and romances*....William Henry, a farmer in Guttorm in

[1] Landstad, *Norske Folkeviser*, note to *Dei Tvo Systar*, p. 867.
[2] *On the Danish Ballads* (*Scottish Historical Review*, Vol. 1, No. 4, July, 1904), p. 362.
[3] *A Tour through Orkney and Schetland in* 1774, Kirkwall, 1879. Cf. also Preface to *Sörla Þáttr*, p. 39 ff. above.
[4] *Ib.*, p. 105 ff.

Foula has the most knowledge of any I found; he spoke of three kinds of poetry used in Norn, and repeated or sung by the old men; the Ballad (or Romance, I suppose); *the Vysie or vyse, now commonly sung to dancers*[1]; and the simple song.... Most of all their tales are relative to the history of Norway; they seem to know little of the rest of Europe but by names; Norwegian transactions they have at their fingers' ends.

One would like to have known more about Norn and its 'Vysies,' which might have formed an interesting and instructive link between some of the Northern ballads. On the other hand, the Scandinavian colonies in Ireland, and settlers in English ports such as Bristol, may have done not a little, through their trade with France and the Mediterranean countries, to spread the new rhyming four line verse and the romantic stories of southern and eastern Europe[2].

While this obscurity remains as to the connection between the Faroese ballads and those of neighbouring countries, notably Denmark, the questions of the age and origin of many of the Faroese ballads in their present form are also frought with difficulty. Of the Danish ballads, which sometimes offer parallels so close as to suggest translation from one language to the other, the first MS. collection that can be dated with certainty was written down in 1550. But there is much evidence, both internal and

---

[1] The *Vyse*, be it observed, is the Danish word most commonly used to denote a ballad. The Faroese use *Kvæði*, and less frequently *Rima*.

[2] For an account of the Scandinavian settlements on the Bristol Channel, cf. A. Bugge, *Contributions to the History of the Norsemen in Ireland*, No. III, published in *Videnskabsselskabet i Christiania, Historisk-filosofisk Klasse*, II, 1900.

external, for assigning a much earlier date to the historical ballads at least. It has been suggested by Olrik[1], who supports his view by arguments which it would be extremely difficult to contest, that many of the historical ballads are practically contemporaneous with the events which they describe, and some of these took place in the thirteenth century, while others, e.g. *Riboldsvisen*, are possibly of the twelfth century.

Unfortunately we have fewer data, whether philological or historical, for assigning dates to the Faroese ballads than we have for the Danish. There can be little doubt, however, that the ballads translated below had their origin in the *Fornaldar Sögur* composed in Iceland during the thirteenth century or in some fourteenth century *Rímur* derived from the sagas. That many of the Faroese ballads were literary in origin[2], and were based on either Sagas or Rímur, is conclusively established by the opening lines of many of the ballads themselves, notably that of the *Olufu Ríma*:

> Ein er ríman ur Íslandi komin,
> Skrívað í bók so breiða.

("This story is come from Iceland, written in a book so broad.")

And *Tröllini í Hornalandum*:

> Verse 1. Frøðíð er komið frá Íslandi
> Skrívað í bók so víða *etc.*

---

[1] Axel Olrik, Introduction to *Danske Folkeviser i Udvalg*, 3rd ed. (Copenhagen and Christiania, 1913), p. 40 ff. Cf. also Steenstrup, *Vore Folkeviser* (Copenhagen, 1891), ch. VII.

[2] On the literary sources of the Faroese ballads, cf. Steenstrup, *op. cit.* Introduction.

Verse 2.   Frøðið er komið frá Íslandi
            Skrívað í bók so breiða *etc.*

Verse 3.   Frøðið er komið frá Íslandi
            Higar ið skald tað tók,
            Havið tær hoyrt um kongin tann,
            Íð skrívaður stendur í bók?

("This poem has come from Iceland, brought hither by a *skald*. Have you heard of the king about whom this book is written?")

The passages quoted above would seem to point to Rímur rather than Sagas as the sources of the ballads. Or had more than one "Book so broad" come from Iceland? One wonders. Heusler notices[1] the tendency to divide up the longer ballads into sections or *Tættir*, each whole in itself and yet forming a part of the ballad, and suggests the Icelandic *Rímur* as the models for this particular form. It is even possible that the word *Ríma* is used advisedly in the first strophe of *Olufu Kvæði*, instead of the somewhat commoner *Kvæði*, with some reminiscence of its origin. One of the *Sjurðar Kvæði* (*Dvörgamoy* III) begins:

Eina veit eg rímuna,
Íð inni hevir ligið leingi.

(I know a rhyme (or *Ríma?*) etc.)

and *Rísin í Holmgarð* also begins:

Eg veit eina rímuna,
Íð gjörd er um Virgar sterka.

Many other instances might be quoted.

But it would be perilous to press too far what may, after all, be a mere verbal coincidence. And whatever

[1] *Lied und Epos* (Dortmund, 1915), p. 19.

gave rise to our poems as they now stand, it cannot be too strongly emphasised that they, like the rest of the *Føroyja Kvæði*, are first and last *Ballads*—rightly ballads. They have a form of their own, like other ballads, and are not a degenerate form of *Rímur* or a mere versification of some old Icelandic legends. Indeed what Professor Ker says of the Danish ballads[1] may with equal truth be applied to the ballads of the Faroes:

The ballads are not rude, rustic travesties of older more dignified stories; though some, perhaps many, of the older stories may survive among the ballads. They are for Denmark in the thirteenth and fourteenth centuries what the older heroic lays of the Poetic Edda had been before them in the Northern lands. They take the place of earlier heroic poetry.

Whatever the nature of their connection with the ballads of the surrounding lands, the Faroese ballads are no isolated growth. They exhibit all the main characteristics of the ballad type, especially of the Danish, Norwegian and Icelandic ballads. Crude and inartistic they often are compared with the best of the Danish and even the Scottish ballads. The *Ballad of Hjalmar and Angantyr* has little to recommend it beyond its simplicity and naïveté, the 'quaintness' of primitive literature; the *Ballad of Arngrim's Sons* exhibits a curious lack of skill in the manipulation of the theme, and perhaps we are justified in assuming that two earlier ballads or perhaps *tættir* have been imperfectly welded. The *Ballad of Nornagest* is bald to a fault and lacks inspiration; and all alike show an imperfect artistry in diction.

[1] *On the History of the Ballads, 1100–1500*, published in *Proceedings of the British Academy* for 1902–1910, p. 202.

Yet despite all these blemishes they are ballads as surely as *Sir Patrick Spens* or *Ungen Sveidal* are ballads. Nor is Professor Ker quite just to the ballads of the Faroes in saying[1] that because of their length, and "because they were made out of books, nothing but the lyrical form and the dancing custom kept them from turning into ordinary romances." Surely no material could be less promising than King Heithrek's Riddles; yet in virtue of what has been forgotten and what has been selected—the telescoping of the riddles and the elaboration of the setting—the ballad spirit has entered in and shaped from the unwieldy mass an artistic whole.

Indeed whatever their faults one realises in all these ballads the truth of Sidgwick's epigram[2]: "You never know what a ballad will say next, though you *do* know how it is going to say it!" For it is even less similarity of theme than similarity of form that links the ballads of the Faroes with those of Denmark and the North. The invariable accompaniment of the refrain; the fluctuation between assonance and rhyme, the disregard of alliteration, and the general verse form; the love of repetition and ballad formulae, —especially of repetition of whole phrases or verses with the alteration of merely the words that rhyme, or of repetition with inversion of word order; the balladist's love of colour, of the material and the concrete, of glitter and shine; the large element of dialogue; the abrupt dramatic openings; the con-densation and concentration of narrative and the

---

[1] *On the History of the Ballads*, etc., p. 202.
[2] Frank Sidgwick, *The Ballad*, London (Arts and Crafts of Letters Series), p. 61.

strict exclusion of the irrelevant or superfluous; the infallible feeling for a 'situation'; the atmosphere of the tragic or the critical; the "echo, without comment, of the clash of man and fate[1]." All these are the elements that make the ballad a form of literature distinct from other lyric or epic forms; all these are the elements that go to make the Faroese ballads what they are—part of what Ker calls the "Platonic Idea, a Ballad in itself, unchangeable and one, of which the phenomenal multitude of ballads are 'partakers[2].'"

[1] Gummere, *The Popular Ballad* (London, 1907), p. 340.
[2] *On the History of the Ballads*, etc., p. 204.

INTRODUCTION TO GRÍPLUR I

In the fourteenth and fifteenth centuries in Iceland, many of the Sagas or portions of them were turned into rhyming verse known as *Rímur*. Sagas of almost every class were subjected to this treatment—*Íslendinga Sögur, Fornaldar Sögur, Fornmanna Sögur* and others. It is supposed that in the first place these rhymed versions (*Rímur*) were made for the purpose of recitation at social gatherings. There is ground for believing that the *Rímur* were sometimes recited, as an accompaniment of dances in Iceland[1]; but this is not believed to have been the purpose for which they were originally composed[2].

According to both Jónsson[3] and Mogk[4], the *Rímur* and other forms of rhyming verse in early Norse poetry originated in the Mediaeval Latin Church Hymns introduced into Iceland in the thirteenth century. The similarity between the rhyming metres of the Latin and many (though not all) of the forms of verse used in the *Rímur* is very striking. Whether the influence of Latin hymns in Iceland was directly responsible for the change, however, as Jónsson and Mogk believe, or whether the Latin hymns only influenced Norse verse indirectly through the medium of French poetry, is

---

[1] Cf. Finnur Jónsson, *Oldnorske og Oldislandske Litteraturs Historie*, Vol. iii, p. 35.

[2] Cf. F. Jónsson, *op. cit.*, Vol. iii, p. 36; also Eugen Mogk, *Geschichte der Norwegisch-Isländischen Literatur* (Strasburg, 1904), p. 722.

[3] *Op. cit.*, iii, p. 26 ff.   [4] *Op. cit.*, p. 722 ff.

problematical. Perhaps these compositions owe
their origin to the fashion of turning all kinds of
material, likely and unlikely, into rhyming verse—
a fashion which originated in France, and from the
latter part of the twelfth century onwards gradually
made its way over most of the West and North of
Europe. The rhyming chronicles of the fourteenth
century in England may be mentioned as one instance of this fashion, and the rhyming paraphrases
of the splendid prose of Iceland are an outcome of
the same movement.

The *Gríplur*, some twenty stanzas of which are
given below, represent this stage in the development
of Icelandic literature. It may be observed that, like
other *Rímur*, they are the work of educated people—
a fact which makes the wretched quality of much of
the verse all the more striking, especially when they
are contrasted with the ballads, which are, at least in
most cases, the work of the unlettered. Unattractive
however as they appear to the modern mind, it has
been thought advisable to include a short extract
from them here because it seems possible that in
some cases the Faroese ballads may have derived
their material from Iceland through the intermediate
stage of the *Rímur* rather than from the Saga direct.

Reference is made to the exploits of Hromund in
other *Rímur* besides the *Gríplur*, notably in the
Málsháttakvæði, the *Skíða-Ríma*[1] (which is interesting
as being based, in all probability, on an earlier poem
than the *Gríplur*) and in the *Klerka-Ríma*[2]. And he

[1] Ed. by K. Maurer, Munich, 1869; F. Jónsson, *Carmina
Scaldica* (Copenhagen. 1913).
[2] Codex A.M. 604 H.

and Thrain the Berserk still live in the popular songs of the North. He is the *Ungen Ranild*¹ of the Danish ballad; and in the Norwegian ballad *Ramund den Unge*², Ramund (Hromund) and Hölgi (Helgi) appear as rivals for the hand of Svanhvit (who, however, is not mentioned by name). Like some of the Faroese ballads on the *Hervarar Saga*, these later versions are far removed from the story as we know it from early Icelandic sources³. They are of interest only to those who care for folk song and ballad for their freshness and their naïve simplicity⁴.

GRÍPLUR I

9. Olaf was a mighty Prince
    Who governed Hörthaland.
    The brave folk dwelling along the coast
    He guarded with his hand.

10. Gnöthar-Asmund, the Prince's father,
    A peerless man was he;
    By many a battle he reft from Kings
    Their land and territory.

11. In the stern of the King's ship Kari stood,
    And of heroes many another;
    In strength of limb had he never a peer;
    And Örnulf was his brother.

¹ S. Grundtvig, *Danmarks Gamle Folkeviser*, Vol. 1, p. 367 ff.

² M. B. Landstad, *Norske Folkeviser* (Christiania, 1853), p. 189 ff.

³ Cf. Kölbing, *Beiträge zur Vergleichenden Geschichte der Romantischen Poesie und Prosa des Mittelalters*, pp. 185–187.

⁴ For further ballads on the story of Hromund Greipsson, cf. Andrews, *Studies in the Fornaldarsögur Northrlanda*, in *Modern Philology*, 1911, 1912.

12. The King and his warriors reddened their swords
    In the blood of wicked men;
    But no man travelling with merchandise
    Got any hurt from them.

13. The Prince brought joy to his followers' hearts,
    With Draupnir's beautiful blood.
    A franklin who better were named a burgess
    Beside the princes stood.

14. Grip was a man who stirred up strife,
    Eager with blade for slaughter.
    This hero's wife was a good woman:
    Of Hrok the Black was she daughter.

15. Grip and Gunnlöth, his good wife,
    They had nine sons in all:
    (Clever verses are made about them)
    And *Hrök* did they every one call!

16. Hromund was a son of Grip,
    Eldest of the brothers was he;
    His heart knew never aught of fear,
    Nor faltered his valiancy.

17. Hrolf must I add, Högni, Haki and Gaut,
    And Thröst with the other five;
    Angantyr and Helgi whose lot it was
    In the fortunes of war to thrive.

18. Logi was youngest (a tiny lad)
    Of the sons of the worthy pair;
    Hromund alone sallied forth to fight in battle,
    And the rest stayed at home where they were.

19. The hero feared neither fire nor sword
    When shields clashed in the fray;
    His shoulders were broad, and shining his hair,
    And kindly and keen was his eye.

20. He never fled or deserted the host,
    But poured forth darts on the shield;—
    Faithful and true in courage was he
    As a hero should be in the field.

21. His wicked foe did he slay with might—
    He knew no fear of pain;
    And all his noble courage and valour
    From his kinsman Hrök did he gain.

22. Two villains were there with the King,
    Deep-versed in magic arts.
    I swear those brothers Bild and Vali
    Both had evil hearts!

23. The King of Vali council takes,
    And a sad mistake made he;
    A name had he gained for courtesy and valour,
    But he never donned byrnie.

24. Less trusty warrior in the field
    I never look to find;—
    False he was and treacherous,—
    Full of deceit his mind.

25. The Prince's troop, the Niflung men,
    Along Norway's coast did sail,
    Until they came to the Skerries of the Elf,—
    Nor did their courage fail.

26. The troop had prepared for a mighty battle,
    And against a promontory
    Olaf's men in their warships there
    Lay at anchor in the bay.

27. "Over the Island do ye go,"—
    Thus to Kari spoke he,—
    "To see if ye come on the vikings' ships,
    And if they are like to fight fiercely."

28. Kari and Ornulf, clothed and armed,
    With shield and polished blade
    Examine the coast, and hastily
    A search through the island made.

29. Six tall warships soon they see,
    Under the sea-cliffs lay they;
    And a '*Dragon*' carved in wondrous wise
    Beside the warships lay.

INTRODUCTION TO THE FAROESE
BALLAD OF NORNAGEST

The *Ballad of Nornagest* was published for the first time by Lyngbye in 1822 in *Færöiske Kvæder om Sigurd Fofnersbane* etc. In his visit to the Faroes in 1847–8, Hammershaimb took down the ballad from oral recitation at Sumbø. He afterwards collated his version carefully with those of Svabo, Schrøter and Lyngbye, and published the result in *Færöiske Kvæder*, Vol. 1, Copenhagen, 1851. This is the version of the ballad translated below.

Lyngbye points out that Nornagest has become a well-known character in modern Faroese legend. We certainly note his popularity in the ballads, which is no doubt due to his association with Sigurth in the original story. In some ballads he appears as a companion in arms of the latter and even as a great warrior himself. He it is who rides with Sigurth and Virgar to meet the giant in Holmgarth (cf. *Rísin í Holmgarðum*, v. 33), and in *Ragnarlikkja* (cf. v. 39 ff.) "the fierce Nornagest" sails with Sigurth, Brand, and Virgar to slay the King of Girtland; and so too in other stories.

It will be observed that the framework of the story differs considerably from that of the Saga, notably in the opening and closing scenes. The beginning of another story, dealing likewise with an old man, has been substituted for the original opening. The mention of the boat in verse 40 is perhaps reminiscent of some folk-tale; and the story of the leaden casket containing the soul of Nornagest which was sunk in the lake is an interesting instance of the external soul. I have no doubt that it is a reference to some folk-tale, but have not yet been able to identify it. Among many primitive peoples, who can hardly grasp abstract ideas, the life or soul of a man is regarded as a concrete thing which can be laid aside, and which, so long as it remains unharmed, will secure for him immortality. There is, for example, a Hindoo story of a princess whose soul was believed to be in her necklace.—One day an astrologer said to her parents: "This is no common child; the necklace of gold about her neck contains your daughter's soul; let it therefore be guarded with the utmost care; for if it were taken off and worn by another person, she would die[1]."

Many similar folk-tales are known from Icelandic and Danish sources as well as from many parts of Europe and Asia.

The air to which the following ballad is sung will be found on pp. 117, 118 of Thuren's *Folkesangen paa Færøerne*.

---

[1] For many interesting parallels, cf. Frazer, *Golden Bough* (London, 1911–1915), "Balder the Beautiful," ch. 11.

Nornagests Rima

Taken down by A. P. BERGGEEN.

Eitt er frøðið um Nor-na gest, - Lat tær rá-ða raðgerð í van-da. - Ti likum góðum gekk hann næst.

Ox-ar tolv voru leid-dir á torg, og so fram á frí-ðu borg. Gra-ni bar gul-lið af heið-ði.

THE FAROESE BALLAD OF NORNAGEST

1. A Ballad there is of Nornagest,
   Refrain:—*Be ready with a plan in trouble!*—
   In manly virtues among the best.
   Refrain:—*Every lad should do so!*

2. Twelve oxen were led to the market square,
   And onward thence to a castle fair.

3. The King he thought to hew them to earth,
   And with courage and joy did he sally forth.

4. The King he struck such a mighty blow
   That the blood from the wounds did swiftly flow.

5. All the oxen fell down dead,
   And the axe sank deep that he brandished.

6. All men praised his princely blow:
   The blood from the wounds did swiftly flow.

7. A man there came with crutches twain:
   With these he steadied himself amain.

8. The King to the man full mildly spoke:—
   "O why, and O why, dost thou praise not my stroke?"

9. "O Sire, thou struckest full manfully;
   But I saw a finer stroke in days gone by.

10. "Of Sigurth's deeds hast thou heard the worth,—
    The mightiest champion of men on earth!

11. "Leaf and grove did tremble and quake
    When Sigurth clove in sunder the snake.

12. "This may you tell of Sigurth the bold:—
    'He was mightiest of all men in days of old.'

13. "This can I tell of Sigurth's fame:—
    'I know no hero with eyes so keen.'

14. "Leaf and grove did tremble and shake
    When Sigurth clove in sunder the snake.

15. "A noble man was Högni, I ween,
    Full well did I know his ugly mien.

16. "Rich, brave and gentle was Gunnar enow,
    Wise too, and Gunnhild was like him, I trow.

17. "Wise too, and Gunnhild was like him, I trow.
    Of heroes like him are there all too few.

18. "My father he had a homestead fair:
    Herds of cattle were pastured there.

19. "And horses I tended as I sat in the wood.—
    And blithest my heart when the weather was good!

20. "One and all in their saddles they ride,
    Childe Sigurth, and Högni, and Gunnar beside.

12—2

22. "Over the mire-pit rode all and one.—
     I was a lad, and I looked thereon.

23. "First sprang Gunnar's horse forthright.
     Gunnar measured his leap aright.

24. "Högni's horse sprang after then.
     Fast stuck Grani in the fen.

25. "The last to spring was Sigurth's steed.
     Sigurth had given him so heavy a feed!

26. "Grani floundered in the fen:
     His saddle girth brake in pieces twain.

27. "Down from their saddles each did glide,—
     Childe Sigurth, and Högni, and Gunnar beside.

28. "They dragged at the noble steed amain;
     But Sigurth pulled hardest the bridal rein.

29. "'Oft have I leapt o'er the pit aright
     By day and eke in the murky night.

30. "'O Guest, a service of thee I pray:—
     Wash from my courser the mire away.

31. "'The saddle buckle which broke 'neath me—
     The same, O Guest, will I give to thee.'

32. "Forth they rode to a river then.
     No-one was there to look to the men.

33. "I washed his poitrail and breast for him,
     His thigh, his leg, and each long limb.

34. "The noble courser I made full clean.
     Then Sigurth took me for his horse-swain.

35. "So rode we forth to Fafnir's lair.
     Like the sun's own beams did the gold shine there.

36. "From Sigurth's steed did I draw a hair,
     Of wondrous length and beyond compare.

37. "The hair in the tail of Grani hung,
     —Well-nigh a foot and a fathom long.

38. "Well-nigh a foot and a fathom in height,
    And it shone and gleamed like silver so bright.

39. "In days gone by, full far have I strayed,
    Nor found I my candle and span of days."

40. The King he gave him pole and boat,
    And directed the old man on his road.

41. "In the Land of the Franks is a lake broad and wide
    Where thy candle and span of days do bide."

42. Long and long dived the courteous man
    Before he came his candle upon.

43. Körnar the priest baptised him anon.
    When the candle burnt out his life was done.

44. When the light in the lanthorn had burnt away,
    Refrain:—*Be ready with a plan in trouble!*—
    Then ended too his own life's day.
    Refrain:—*Every lad should do so!*

INTRODUCTION TO THE BALLAD OF HJALMAR AND ANGANTYR

The following ballad was taken down by Hammershaimb from oral recitation in Westmanhavn in 1846, and published at Copenhagen in 1855 in *Færöiske Kvæder*, Vol. ii. He took down a second version of the same ballad, but consisting of only nineteen stanzas, at Sumbø in 1847, which he published in the *Antiquarisk Tidsskrift*, 1849–50. This second version differs slightly from the one given in our text. In it Arngrim is said to have twelve sons of whom Angantyr was the youngest. Hjalmar is not expressly stated to have been a brother of Angantyr, as he is in our version and in the Danish ballad *Angelfyr and Helmer the Warrior* (cf. p. 188 ff.). Moreover Angantyr is the first to learn of the franklin's daughter, and he forthwith builds a ship and sails away alone; and it is only later that Hjalmar also hears of her and sets sail, thus reaching the spot when Angantyr has already landed. More colour is given to the maiden's choice in the second version by the additional detail that

> Hjalmar leapt so lightly to land,
> He made no footprint on the sand.

This, however, it is to be noted, is the regular formula by which the landing of the hero is described in the Faroese ballads. Cf. *Lokka Táttur*, v. 78.

It is the opinion of Hammershaimb that this ballad was the original from which the longer ballad of *Arngrim's Sons* sprang. This would seem to be supported by Heusler's contention that *The Long Ballad* of the *Marsk Stig* Cycle was composed by welding together several shorter ballads[1]; and certainly the *Ballad of Arngrim's Sons* suggests that at least two distinct ballads have been run into one, especially when we compare the two varying versions of Svabo and Hammershaimb. Against this, however, we have to place the fact that something of the same invertebrate impression is given by the *Saga of Hervör and Heithrek*, on which these ballads are ultimately based. Even if we assume a composite origin for the *Ballad of Arngrim's Sons*, there is no evidence that any portion of it was based on the short *Ballad of Hjalmar and Angantyr*, while the difference of metre diminishes the probability of a connection.

The air and refrain to this ballad are given on p. 124 of Thuren's *Folkesangen paa Færøerne*.

---

[1] *Lied und Epos* (Dortmund, 1905), p. 41 ff.

The Ballad of Hjalmar and Angantyr

KIRKJUBØ.

Bóndin undir eikini byr, - Væl bornir
menn - Eigir hann ellivu synir dýr! - Arngríms
synir á Bjarn - londum ber - jast við Sams oy.

THE BALLAD OF HJALMAR AND
ANGANTYR

1. A man lived up in a high oak-tree,
    Refrain:—   *Ye well-born men!*—
    Eleven warlike sons had he.
    Refrain:—   *Arngrim's Sons from Africa,*
                    They fought, they fought on Samsø.

2. He had eleven sons so dear,—
    The champions Hjalmar and Angantyr.

3. A ship, a ship did these warriors man,
    And swift 'fore the wind was the course she ran.

4. They hoisted their sail to the mast so high:
    They had faith in their strength and their valiancy.

5. Their anchor they cast in the white, white sand.
    Hjalmar hastily sprang to the land.

6. Their anchor they cast in the white, white sand.
   And Angantyr eagerly sprang on the strand.

7. Angantyr eagerly sprang on the strand.
   Up to his knees he sank in the sand.

8. "I drew my hose from my legs so bare
   To hide the sand from my lady fair!"

9. In the garden they busked them in cloaks of skin,
   And so went up to the franklin sitting there within.

10. "Here sittest thou, franklin, drinking thy wine:
    I beg that thy daughter so fair may be mine!"

11. When Hjalmar stood before the board,
    Angantyr straight took up the word.—

12. "Here sittest thou, franklin, drinking thy wine:
    I beg that thy daughter so fair may be mine!"

13. In sorry plight was the franklin then,
    For there at the board stood two mighty men.

14. "No choice so hard will I ever make;
    The maiden herself must choose her mate."

15. "No choice so hard shall be made by thee:
    The warrior Hjalmar shall wed with me.

16. "With Hjalmar the Brave would I wedded be,
    Who is so lovely and fair to see."

17. "O franklin! Lend me a trusty blade,
    We two must fight for the hand of the maid."

18. "O franklin! Lend me a sharp penknife:
    Each of us surely must lose his life."

19. They fought their way forth of the hall.
    They bellowed louder than any troll.

20. Till they reached a river they fought amain,
    Down on their knees and then up again.

21. Down on their knees and then up again
    Refrain:—   *Ye well-born men!*—
    Till stiff and dead lay those champions twain.
    Refrain:—   *Arngrim's Sons from Africa,*
                       They fought, they fought on Samsø.

INTRODUCTION TO THE DANISH
BALLAD OF ANGELFYR AND
HELMER THE WARRIOR

Four different versions of the Danish ballad of *Angelfyr and Helmer the Warrior* are given by Grundtvig in *Danmarks Gamle Folkeviser*, Vol. 1, number 19 (Copenhagen, 1853). Two of these, closely allied, are found in a MS. written in the sixteenth century[1]. The version which Grundtvig has called *A* is the one adopted for translation below.

An interesting study in ballad composition is afforded by a comparison of this Danish ballad with the Faroese ballads of the *Sons of Arngrim*. According to Axel Olrik[2] the Danish ballad is founded on the *Saga of Hervör and Heithrek*. That the ultimate source of all the ballads of the *Sons of Arngrim* was the Saga there can be no doubt. But whether the Danish ballad is derived directly from the Saga or through some intermediate stage, Icelandic, Faroese or Danish, is problematical. A definite relationship between the Danish and the Faroese ballads would seem to be shown by several common features of the story which do not occur in the Saga itself, as well as by some striking verbal resemblances which have no foundation in the prose narrative.

[1] Cf. Grundtvig, *Danmarks Gamle Folkeviser*, Vol. 1, p. 252. Also Axel Olrik, *Danske Folkeviser i Udvalg*, Vol. 1, p. 263.

[2] Cf. Olrik, *op. cit.*, p. 78. For general information on the Danish ballads the reader is referred to Steenstrup, *Vore Folkeviser* (Copenhagen, 1891), translated by E. G. Cox (Boston, 1914).

Thus on the one hand both in the Danish and in the Faroese ballads translated above, Hjalmar and Angantyr are described as brothers[1], whereas in the Saga they are not related. On the other hand the Danish and the two Faroese ballads are almost identical in their description of Angantyr and all his kin as "vile trolls," though Version *A* given by Grundtvig describes him in accordance with the Saga as a "half-troll" (i.e. on his mother's side).

Other close verbal parallels, surely indicative of cross-relationship or of a common source, are afforded by a comparison of certain passages of the Danish ballad and the Faroese *Ballad of Arngrim's Sons*. Thus *v.* 5 of the Danish is practically identical with *v.* 74 of the Faroese, and we may compare *v.* 9 of the shorter *Ballad of Hjalmar and Angantyr*. May we also compare *v.* 6 of the Danish with *v.* 79 of the longer Faroese ballad; *v.* 8 with *v.* 81; *v.* 10 with *v.* 84; *v.* 14 with *v.* 79? Conventional as many of these phrases are, the identity can hardly be accidental in all cases.

The precise nature of the relationship between the two versions is not so clear. We may note, however, some of the features contained in the Danish version of the story which are not found in the Saga. In the first place neither Arngrim nor Samsø are mentioned, the names Offue and Uthiss-kier being substituted for them[2]; secondly, except in the refrain there is no mention of the sea or a voyage in the Danish ballad. Helmer bids them "saddle his steed," and both he

[1] See, however, the Introduction to the *Ballad of Hjalmar and Angantyr*, p. 182 above.

[2] So MS. *A*; but cf. below *v.* 1 and note.

and Angelfyr *ride* to Upsala. Finally after *v.* 11 of our text, the Danish ballad differs entirely from the Faroese version of the story and also from that of the *Saga of Hervör and Heithrek*. Offue's revenge is peculiar to the Danish, and here too no mention is made of Ingibjörg's death.

From all these changes, and especially from the transference of names and places, it is obvious that the Danish version of the story is considerably more remote from the Saga than either of the two Faroese versions. At the same time, the absence of any reference to Samsø or any other Danish locality renders it highly improbable that its divergences are due to any (Danish) local tradition independent of the Saga.

On the whole it would seem that at an early date (fifteenth or early sixteenth century?) a ballad had been made from this portion of the Saga, either directly or through the intermediate stage of a lost rhymed version; and that it was composed in the Faroes themselves or in Iceland or some other region —the Orkneys and Shetlands are a possible suggestion—and acquired by the Danes not very long afterwards.

ANGELFYR AND HELMER THE WARRIOR

1. Offue he dwelt in Uthiss-kier,
       Both rich and bold was he;
    And when two sons were born to him,
       He vowed they should warriors be.

Refrain: *But the tempest from the North*
             Lashes dark and troubled billows
             On the gleaming waste of sand[1].

2. It was Young Helmer the Warrior;
       He bade them saddle his steed:
    "I Ride to Upsala this day,
       The King's daughter to wed."

3. Then up and spake Young Angelfyr,
       Where he stood in scarlet so red:
    "O never shalt thou this eventide
       To the lovely maid be wed!"

4. Then up and spake Young Angelfyr:
       He bade them saddle his steed:
    "I will gallop today to Upsala,
       Till the earth is rent with my speed."

5. Out of doors in the castle-court
       They busked them in cloaks of skin,
    And so went they to the hall gallery,
       Where the King of Upsala sat within.

6. In came Young Helmer the Warrior,
       And stood before the board;
    "O King, I pray thee, give me thy daughter,—
       I wait thy friendly word."

7. In there came Young Angelfyr,
       And gold shone on his hand:
    "O King, I pray thee, give me thy daughter
       And quit thee from this thy land."

8. Long and long stood the King of Upsala,
       And pondered silently,
    How those heroes who stood before him
       He might answer fittingly.

[1] The translation of the refrain is somewhat free; but cf. Olrik,
D. F. i U., p. 78. Extreme condensation is a feature of all Faroese
and Danish ballad refrains which makes a literal translation into
English practically impossible.

9. It was the King of Upsala,
   And he spake this word theretil:
   "I give my daughter to that man only
   Who has won him her goodwill."

10. "I give thee thanks, my father dear,
    That the choice thou lay'st on me;
    I give myself to Young Helmer the Warrior,
    For a noble man is he.

11. "I will not wed me to Angelfyr:
    For he is half a troll;—
    So is his father, and so his mother,
    And so are his kinsfolk all."

12. Then up and spake Young Angelfyr
    As he stood and pondered there:
    "We both will take us forth to the courtyard,
    And fight for the maiden fair."

13. It was the King of Upsala,
    And answered he forthright:
    "O the swords they be keen, and the lads they be bold,
    And may measure them well in a fight."

14. Then up and rose Young Angelfyr
    Where he his sword out drew;
    And up rose Young Helmer the Warrior,
    Whom he to the earth did hew.

15. Offue he stands in Uthiss-kier
    And far and wide looks he:
    "O somewhere is Helmer suffering pain,
    For I feel such woe in the heart of me."

16. Offue he stands in Uthiss-kier
    And looks o'er the wide, wide heath:
    "O what can be harming my two sons today,
    And why are they both so wroth?"

17. It was Offue in Uthiss-kier;
    He sprang on his red-roan steed.
    And so came he to the King's courtyard,
    Ere Helmer was dead indeed.

18. "O hearken, hearken, Young Helmer,
    Beloved son of mine:
    Thy noble sword from out thy hands
    Why didst thou list to tine?"

19. "Eight are the mortal wounds I bear,
    They are both deep and sore;
    And had I only one of them
    I could not live an hour."

20. O it was Offue in Uthiss-kier,
    And he his sword out drew;—
    And O it was Young Angelfyr
    Whom down to the earth he slew.

21. "Lie thou there, Young Angelfyr,
    And bleed till thou art dead;
    So woeful was I in my heart
    When I saw how Helmer bled.

22. "Lie thou there, Young Angelfyr,
    And lose thy life-blood all.
    So woeful was I in my heart
    When I saw Young Helmer fall."

Refrain: *But the tempest from the North
            Lashes dark and troubled billows
            On the gleaming waste of sand.*

In MS. *B* of the *Ballad of Angelfyr* etc., *vv.* 1–11
correspond pretty closely to MS. *A*; but *vv.* 12–18
are different:

12. Alff he stood in Odderskier,
    And listened over the field;
    Then could he hear so far away
    Where his sons their swords did wield.

13. Up then rose Alff in Odderskier;
    He sprang on his red-roan steed;
    And came he so to Upsala
    Ere both the warriors were dead.

14. "O hearken, hearken, Young Helmer,
         Beloved son of mine:
     Why does the life blood from thy head
         In streams come running down?"

15. It was Young Helmer the Warrior,
         And his father answered he:
     "My brother Angelfyr could not have the maid,
         And therefore he wrought this ill to me.

16. "My body is pierced with fifteen wounds,
         All tainted with poison full sore;
     And had I only one of them
         I could not live an hour."

17. It was Alff in Odderskier,
         And an oak he uprootéd;
     He struck with the oak Young Angelfyr,
         Till he lay on the earth stone dead.

18. Now both these warriors are lying dead,
         And dead lie they in their grave;
     And the King he is ready to give his daughter
         To the man whom he himself will have.

INTRODUCTION TO THE FAROESE
BALLAD OF ARNGRIM'S SONS

The *Ballad of Arngrim's Sons* was first taken down by Svabo towards the close of the eighteenth century. He never published it, but his MS. (III. 9) is preserved in the Royal Library at Copenhagen. In 1848 V. U. Hammershaimb took the ballad down again from oral recitation on Sandø and published it in the *Antiquarisk Tídsskrift*, 1849–1851 (Copenhagen, 1852). He had, however, consulted Svabo's version, for he says in the prefatory note to the ballad:

It is entirely confused in Svabo's version in the Royal Library. I have therefore kept to the version which I got on Sandø, which in the main points agrees with the Saga. Only in the conclusion and two other passages have I followed Svabo's version.

By 1855, however, it would seem that his view had changed. In his prefatory note to the *Ballad of Arngrim's Sons*, published in *Nordiske Oldskrifter*, vols. 18–19, Part II (Copenhagen, 1855), he writes:

The version given by Svabo is at variance with the Saga and has many internal discrepancies arising mainly from the fact that Hjalmar and Angantyr are here taken to be brothers, as in the Danish ballad. In the *Antiquarisk Tídsskrift* for 1849–1851 I published another version which I took down in Sandø in 1848, and in which I made some use of Svabo's version. My version corresponds exactly with the *Harvarar Saga*, but it is open to suspicion from the fact that it here forms the second part (*tháttr*) of *Hjalmar's Kvæði*, of which the first part (*The Tháttr of Örvar-Oddr*) is clearly of later origin; as is shown not only by the language, but also by the fact that the whole falls in with Suhm's story,—"The three friends, Hjalmar, Asbjörn and Örvarodd," etc. Many verses of *Arngrim's Sons* presuppose a first *táttur* to the ballad, for example that in which the sick Asbjörn complains that he cannot follow his companion to the fight on Samsø[1]. That the language in the second part is purer and older than in the first part is easily explained from the fact that the people of Sandø have utilised the older Faroese version which was taken down by Svabo. They only needed to transpose the verses and to make a very few changes to get the whole readjusted according to the Saga or Suhm's story. The verses which the Sandø version has in common with Svabo's could therefore be used for purposes of comparison. There are thus weighty reasons for giving preference to Svabo's version, in spite of all its imperfections.

Of the first part of *Hjalmar's Kvæði* I have unfortunately been unable to obtain a copy, though it is no doubt accessible at Copenhagen, as it is mentioned as number 60 ('*Hjalmar's Kvæði*, 2 tættir: *a*, Örvaroddur, *b*, Arngrim's Sinir') in a list of Faroese ballads taken down in the Faroes by Hammershaimb for the archaeological archives of the Royal Old Norse Text Society[2]. Hammershaimb says[3], however, that the first part "deals with Hjalmar's youth, the counsel given him by his father when he leaves home, how he is taken into the retinue (*hirð*) of the Swedish King, how he distinguishes himself by his bravery against the vikings,

[1] Cf. also the introduction of Örvar-Odd in v. 29 of Hammershaimb's version (*Antiq. Tidss.*, 1849–51, pp. 61–74); also vv. 28, 33, 58.
[2] Cf. *Antiq. Tidss.*, 1849–1851, p. 28.
[3] *Ib.*, p. 58.

and how he and Asbjörn and Örvarodd swear to be foster-brothers."

The translation which follows is made from Hammershaimb's second edition of the ballad, published in *Nordiske Oldskrifter*, vols. 18 and 19, Part II[1]— which is in fact Svabo's text; but the refrain of his first version has been adopted.

It will be noticed that the ballad differs in many points from the *Saga of Hervör and Heithrek*. In the first place, according to the ballad, it is Arngrim and not Angantyr who is buried with the sword Tyrfing[2]. Secondly, Hervik (the Hervör of the Saga) is described as a daughter of Arngrim and a sister of Angantyr. Hjalmar also is a brother of Hervik and of Angantyr according to the ballad, and actually accompanies Hervik on her quest of the sword Tyrfing, which according to the ballad took place *before* the fight on Samsø. Finally, Arngrim is said to have been killed by Örvarodd, and Hervik accordingly kills Örvarodd in retaliation. Another 'Young Odd' appears later as Hjalmar's companion in the true place of Örvarodd.

Thus we see that, as commonly happens in popular poetry, complex situations have become simplified, and, where simplification has not taken place, the people and events have become confused[3]. Both in the shorter Faroese ballad of *Hjalmar and Angantyr*, and in the Danish ballad of *Angelfyr and Helmer the*

---

[1] Copenhagen, 1855.

[2] So Svabo's version; the Sandø version of Hammershaimb's first edition, however, preserves Angantyr here.

[3] A still more striking instance of the latter development will be found in the *Gátu Ríma* (see p. 213 f. below) especially v. 22.

Warrior, the simplification has proceeded even farther, and a still more striking instance of rigorous simplification is to be found in the *Ballad of Nornagest*.

No *Rímur* dealing with Arngrim's Sons have been published, and I have not been able to ascertain whether any exist, though a passing mention is made of them in verse 74 of the satirical poem *Skíthar íma*[1], probably composed in the fifteenth century by Einar or Sigurður Fóstri. *A priori* it would seem probable that the ballads are derived from compositions of this kind rather than from the Saga direct. But it would be unwise to hazard even a guess as to the balance of probability without detailed knowledge of the relative circulation, distribution and popularity of the Sagas and the Rímur respectively.

The air to which the following ballad is sung on the Faroes has been transcribed and printed by Thuren in *Folkesangen paa Færøerne*, pp. 132, 133.

The Ballad of Arngrim's Sons

♩. = 116   SANDOY.

Arngrímur   eigir   eina borg, hon   stendur   á
ellivu   eigir   hann   synir   sær og   tólvti   er

Refrain

högum   fjalli,   Nú   fellur   rí   man   yvir tann
riddarín   snjalli.

---

[1] *Carmina Scaldica* (*a selection of Norwegian and Icelandic Scaldic poetry*) by Finnur Jónsson, Copenhagen, 1913.

breiða   fjörð;   har   liggur   ein   bón - di

deyður í   dökkari   jörd!   Nú   fellur   rí - man.

Variations of Refrain of

The Ballad of Arngrim's Sons

(1)   I SØRVAGI.

KVALBØ.

THE BALLAD OF ARNGRIM'S SONS.

1.   High on a lofty mountain
      Does Arngrim his castle hold;
    He has eleven noble sons,
      And his twelfth is a champion bold.

Refrain: *Noble men are sailing now from Norway,*
        And a fair breeze bears them o'er the wave.

2   He has eleven noble sons,
      Each skilled to wield his brand;
    And mightiest of all is Angantyr
      Who comes from Bjarnaland.

3. He has eleven noble sons,
      Beneath oak-trees live they;
   And Angantyr lives with them there
      And a warrior bold is he.

4. Arngrim and the Earl's lady,
      Children so fine had they—
   Their daughter was named Hervik,
      Who governed land and fee.

5. This maiden was named Hervik,
      'Fore all men I declare,
   She tilted in the tourney
      When the lads were playing there.

6. She tilted in the tourney
      Among the lads so strong.
   Then blood was up and blood was shed
      Ere she had played her long.

7. Down then sat the lads there;
      Angry were they each one.—
   "Better than fighting us so fiercely
      Go 'venge thy father anon!"

8. Water she cast on her armour;
      She list no longer to fight,
   But went and stood before her mother,
      With cheeks all red and white.

9. "O hearken, hearken my Mother dear,
      The truth from thee would I know.—
   Was my father slain in battle
      Or did he die on straw?"

10. "No truer tale can I tell to thee,
       My daughter whom I love:
    He fell before the bold Örvarodd
       To the South in Isan's Grove.

11. "I can tell thee no truer, my daughter dear
       Than I tell as here I stand;—
    He fell before the bold Örvarodd
       To the South in Isan's Land."

12. She took her quickly to a chest
      Which guarded gold and fee;
    She drew a shirt from out the chest,
      And flung it on Hervik's knee.

13. She drew a shirt from out the chest,
      All bloodstained where it had lain.—
    "Here may'st thou see the very same shirt
      In which thy father was slain."

14. Up then rose Hervik the Earl's daughter
      And manned ship hastily;
    Its cables were of shining gold,
      All twisted cunningly.

15. Up then rose Hervik the Earl's daughter,
      And decked her ship so fine,
    And bade them store within the hold
      Both ale and costly wine.

16. Tarred were the masts,
      And black was the ship in hue;
    The masthead was of the red, red gold,
      And the sun shone on it too.

17. Tarred were the masts;
      The ship it was quite new;
    The golden weather-cock spun aloft,
      And shone amid Heaven's own blue.

18. Tarred were the masts,
      The beams scored wondrously;
    Stem and stern were of red, red gold,
      And so was the sail on high.

19. All in the middle of the ship's deck
      The colour shone so fair
    Where Hervik, the Earl's daughter,
      Sat on the platform there.

20. She hoists aloft her silken sail,
      Striped gold on a scarlet ground,
    Nor ever once does she strike it again
      Till she comes to Isan's Land.

21. She hoists aloft her silken sail,
         (The like will scarce be found)
     Nor ever once does she strike it again
         Till she comes to Isan's ground.

22. Forth when Hervik's frigate
         Touched the fair land,
     Cast she forth her anchor
         Into the white, white sand.

23. Cast she down her anchor
         Into the white, white sand;
     And the first was Hervik the Earl's daughter
         To spring with her foot to land.

24. The first was Hervik the Earl's daughter
         To spring with her foot to land,
     And with her Hjalmar her brother
         Close at her right hand.

25. There a huntsman met her;
         He had hunted herd and fee:
     "O why art thou so sorrowful,
         As a troll had been hunting thee?"

26. Then up stood Hervik the Earl's daughter,
         Her good sword out she drew,
     And with it she clove the huntsman
         And him in sunder slew

27. Three cross roads are bending,
         And one can she descry;
     Hervik has gone straight forth to the barrow
         Wherein her father doth lie.

28. Hervik has gone straight forth to the barrow
         Where her father lies dead and cold.
     Little recks she of fear or favour,
         Though quake now fell and fold.

29. Then up and spake the voice of Arngrim,
         And these words first spake he:—
     "O where are my eleven sons gone,
         Since daughters are visiting me?"

30. "I pass not for my eleven brothers,
    Or where they share their fee.
    No treasure have I, save only Hjalmar,
    Hither brought with me.

31. "O haste thee, haste thee, my noble Father
    The good brand to give me;
    Or shall I set fire here to this barrow,
    And burn it over thee?"

32. Full woe was the champion Arngrim
    That she should wreck his grave.
    He seizéd Tyrfing in both his hands
    And to his daughter gave.

33. He gave to her the sword then
    Was wonderfully made.—
    The length of it was eighteen ells,
    And poisoned was its blade.

34. He gave to her the sword then
    Was wonderfully made.
    No leechcraft could avail the man
    Was wounded by its blade.

35. All in the middle of the garden
    She clad her in cloak of skin;
    She busked her in a cloak of fur,
    And entered the high hall within.

36. She busked her in her cloak of fur
    And entered the high hall belive,
    Where Örvarodd sat before the board
    With a hundred men and five.

37. "O welcome, welcome, Hervik,
    Hither now to me
    Mead or wine shalt thou have to drink
    As liefest is to thee."

38. "O little to me is thy mead, Örvarodd,
    And little to me thy wine.
    Today I have come to thy high hall,
    And a different errand is mine.

39.   "O little to me is thy mead, Örvarodd,
          And little to me thy beer;
      For a different errand did I busk me
          When I left my home to come here.

40.   "I busked me and came from Sweden
          To fight in this thy land.
      Stand up! Stand up! Thou bold Örvarodd,
          Stand up, and arm thy band!"

41.   It fell full early on a morning tide,
          Before the sun rose high,
      Bold Örvarodd had a hundred men and twelve
          Accoutred royally.

42.   Bold Örvarodd had a hundred men and twelve
          Accoutred royally.
      Then up rose Hervik, the Earl's daughter,
          To meet them gallantly.

43.   Up then rose Hervik, the Earl's daughter,
          So doughty in the fight.
      She blew a blast on her golden horn,
          And struck to left and right.

44.   It was Hervik, the Earl's daughter,
          So gallantly she rode;—
      She clove to the shoulders every knight
          Who forth against her strode.

45.   She clove to the shoulders every knight
          Who forth against her strode,
      Till only Örvarodd and his two companions
          Survivors of the army stood.

46.   Under the castle gateway
          The King crept fearfully.—
      "Now mercy, mercy, sweet Hervik,
          I pray thou'lt give to me!"

47.   "Just so much is the sweet mercy
          Thou now shalt get of me
      As thou gavest to my noble Father
          When thou slew'st him felonly!"

48. "Just so much is the sweet mercy
    Thou now shalt win of me
    As thou gavest to my noble Father
    When thou slew'st him cruelly!"

49. That was Hervik, the Earl's daughter,
    To draw her sword was fain.
    She has slain the warrior Örvarodd
    And cut him in pieces twain.

50. She has slain the warrior Örvarodd
    And cut him in pieces twain,
    And all his men so brave and true
    She has heaped on his corse amain.

51. Up then rose Hervik, the Earl's daughter;
    Through the greenwood gan she ride;
    But hawk or hound made never a cry
    In the greenwood by her side.

52. She hoists aloft her silken sail,
    Striped gold on a scarlet ground;
    Nor ever once does she strike it again
    Till she reaches far Uppland.

53. Forth when Hervik's frigate
    Touched the fair land,
    Cast she forth her anchor
    Into the white, white sand.

54. Cast she forth her anchor
    Into the white, white sand;
    And forthwith her brother Angantyr
    Came riding down the strand.

55. She gave to him the sword then
    Was wonderfully made.—
    The length of it was eighteen ells,
    And poisoned was its blade.

56. She gave to him the sword then
    Was wonderfully made.—
    No leechcraft could avail the man
    Was wounded by its blade.

57. Angantyr sits in his high seat,
        And with his men spake he!—
     "O where will I get a make to myself?
        This thought has been long with me."

58. One and all they hung their heads,
        And never a word spake they,
     Save Hjalmar his brother, and better were it
        He had held his peace that day.

59. "I can no truer tell thee,
        But and thou list to hear:
     The King of Upsala has a daughter,
        And she is passing fair.

60. "The King of Upsala has a daughter
        As lovely as the sun.
     Her cheeks they are as red and white
        As blood on driven snow.

61. "The King of Upsala has a daughter:
        Of many is her fame the word.
     Her throne it is of the red, red gold,
        And stands at the King's own board."

62. "O gin the maiden be so fair,
        And gin she be so fine,
     I swear an oath, though ill betide,
        To call that maiden mine.

63. "O long and long will the journey be
        O'er breaker but and billow;
     But I go forth to Upsala, Hjalmar,
        And thou, my brother, must follow."

64. Then up spake Hjalmar the warrior,
        And straightway answered he:
     "The bird feels joy when he spies a corpse,
        And so do I follow thee!"

65. Up then rose him Angantyr,
        And manned ship hastily.
     Its cables were of shining gold
        All twisted cunningly.

66. Up then rose him Angantyr,
    And decked his ship so fine,
    And bade them store within the hold
    Both ale and costly wine.

67. He hoists aloft his silken sail,
    Striped gold on a scarlet ground
    Nor ever once does he strike it again
    Till he comes to Uppsaland.

68. Forth then when his frigate
    Touched the fair land,
    Cast he down his anchor
    Into the white, white sand.

69. Cast he down his anchor
    Into the white, white sand.
    And Angantyr was the first to light
    With his foot to land.

70. Angantyr was the first to light
    With his foot to land,
    And by him Hjalmar his brother,
    Close at his right hand.

71. By him Hjalmar his brother
    Close at his right hand;
    Truly is it told to me
    He sank to his knees in sand.

72. Up they went from the sea-shore,
    Those men of wealth and worth;
    The rollers brake, and the earth it shook
    As they set their ships in berth.

73. Up they went from the sea-shore,
    In their clothes of scarlet so fair;
    Their helmets were of burnished gold,
    And no man did they fear.

74. All in the middle of the garden
    They clad them in cloaks of skin;
    They busked them in their cloaks of fur
    And entered the high hall within.

75. They busked them in their cloaks of fur
         And entered the high hall belive,
     Where the King of Uppland sat at the board
         With a hundred men and five.

76. Hjalmar went into the high hall
         With silk embroidered hood.
     His cheeks were red as lobster's claws,
         His eyes were like the dove.

77. Angantyr has do'en him to the high hall,
         'Twas the custom in days gone by;
     And all in a word did he hail the King
         And ask for the maid truly.

78. Angantyr stands on the hall floor,
         Offers him greeting there;—
     "Now hail be to thee, bold King of Uppsaland,
         Give me thy daughter fair!"

79. Then up and spake the bold Hjalmar,
         Before the broad board he stood:—
     "O King, I pray thee, give me thy daughter
         Who is so fair and good."

80. Up then rose the bold Hjalmar,
         Before the broad board sat he:—
     "O King, I pray thee, give me thy daughter
         Who is so wise and fair to see."

81. Long in sorrow sat the King
         And silently pondered.
     What he should answer the two fierce warriors,
         Who stood before the board.

82. Up then rose the King of Uppsaland;
         Angry and wroth was he:
     "My lady daughter shall come to the hall
         And for herself reply."

83. They have led his daughter to the hall,
         Attended fittingly;
     And Hjalmar's face grew red and pale
         As in the high-seat sat he.

84. "Now thanks and thanks to my noble father
Who gave this choice to me.
Hjalmar the champion from Uppland,
He shall my husband be.

85. "I will not wed me to Angantyr:
He is so vile a troll;
So is his father and so his mother,
And so are his kinsfolk all."

86. "Come forth, come forth, thou bold Hjalmar
For ne'er so brief a tide.
To battle on an island make thee bowne;
She shall not be thy bride."

87 Then up and answered Odd the Young:
"Once more we are fighting here.
You shall go against Arngrim's Sons,
And I against Angantyr."

88. "We two, Angantyr and I,
Shall fight with mighty strife;
I would not that lady Ingibjörg hear
That I sought to flee for my life.

89. "We two, Angantyr and I,
Shall meet in a mighty gripe,
And long will lady Ingibjörg wait
Ere she hear that I shrank for my life."

90. Out then spake the Young Odd,
And pondered heavily;
"O gin thou go'est against Angantyr,
Thou choosest thy death truly."

91. All the sons of Arngrim
Rode up the river shore
A-tightening of their shield-straps
Till they could tighten them no more.

92. All the sons of Arngrim
Rode through the plain so green;
A league and a league you could hear on the stones
The clang of their spears so keen.

93. All the sons of Arngrim,
        Angry were they in mood.
     Little recked they for weapons,
        But tore up clubs of stout oakwood.

94. All the sons of Arngrim
        Rode up the river strand.
     It is the young Odd will lose his life,
        For Hjalmar is not at hand.

95. Odd rode against the Sons of Arngrim,
        His noble weapons proved he so,
     And he slew all the eleven brothers
        Yet never dealt he a second blow.

96. Angantyr and the bold Hjalmar
        On the island combated.
     All their followers who manned the ship
        Are lying now stone dead.

97. Hjalmar then struck Angantyr,
        So lay he at his feet.
     "O Hjalmar, give me now a drink,
        For it comforts the meanest wight."

98. "A drink from out my drinking horn
        I give thee willingly;
     But hearken, Angantyr my brother,
        Today have I surely conquered thee."

99. O he held the horn before his lips,
        —He the noble warrior,—
     And O it was the heathen dog
        Who stabbed him under the helmet there.

100. It was the warrior Hjalmar,
        He drew his sword amain;
     He has cleft his brother Angantyr
        And cut him in pieces twain.

101. Odd came home at eventide
        A-riding on the strand,
     And saw where Hjalmar had sat him there,
        Marred by the poisoned brand.

K.   14

102.   Odd came home at eventide,
            Where Hjalmar leant his back on a stone;
        "O why art thou so wondrous pale,
            And what has brought thee to make such moan?"

103.   "My corslet he has piercéd,
            He has scathed my skin so white;
        The poison smeared upon the blade
            My heart will surely smite."

104.   "Thou didst put thy faith in thy corslet,
            All made of shining steel;
        But here stand I in my shirt only,
            And yet no wound I feel.

105.   "Thou didst put thy trust in thy corslet,
            All made of silver bright;
        But here stand I in my shirt only,
            And got no wound in the fight.

106.   "Thou did'st put thy trust in thy corslet,
            All made of silver white;
        But here stand I in my shirt only
            Which sword could never bite."

107.   Then up and spake the Warrior Hjalmar.
            The first word he did say
        Was "Hearken and hearken now Young Odd,
            And bear me hence away."

108.   Then up and answered the Young Odd,
            He gazed on the rocky ravine:
        "This fight, O Hjalmar, if thou list to hear
            Has gone as I had foreseen."

109.   He drew the gold ring from his arm;
            Speech could he utter still;
        Bade carry it to the lady Ingibjörg,
            And bade him fare him well

110.   He drew the gold ring from his arm;
          All floating was he in blood.
       He sent it to the lady Ingibjörg,
          That maid so fair and good.

111.   She died of grief for Hjalmar—
          She the noble maid;
       I swear an oath upon my honour
          There lives none of whom the like can be said.

   Refrain: *Noble men are sailing now from Norway,*
                 And a fair breeze bears them o'er the wave.

INTRODUCTION TO THE FAROESE RIDDLE BALLAD (GÁTU RÍMA)

The *Gátu Ríma* was first taken down in Suderø by
a clergyman, Schröter, early in the nineteenth century,
and is preserved in the archives of the Early Text
Society in Copenhagen. Unfortunately Schröter was
only able to obtain the Ballad in a fragmentary form,
and he has left us only a Danish translation of what
he found. In his travels on the Faroes in 1847–1848
Hammershaimb made strenuous efforts to get the
entire version, but curiously enough only succeeded
in getting a version (of course in the original
Faroese) which corresponds closely in length and
content with Schröter's. He published this version
first in the *Antiquarisk Tidsskrift*, 1849–1851, and
later in *Færöiske Kvæðer*, vol. II. (Copenhagen, 1855).
The translation given below is taken from the ballad
as printed in *Færöiske Kvæðer*.

That a longer version of this ballad once existed
is proved by the fact that verse 8 of both Schröter's
and Hammershaimb's versions states that Guest the
Blind[1] propounds thirty riddles to King Heithrek—
about the same number as are to be found in the Saga,
though only some six riddles and the answers to
four others have come down to us. Hammershaimb
attributed the loss of the others to the fact that the
ballad is no longer one of those used in the dance.

---

[1] Presumably a corruption of *Gestumblindi*.

He was of opinion that the riddles propounded in the *Ríma* are not the same as those found in the Saga; but it is to be noticed that the subjects of the riddles are in four cases the same, and in the other cases the subjects have the same characteristics, though the riddles themselves are not identical. It would therefore seem on the whole that the subjects of the *Gátu Ríma* were originally identical with those of the Saga, but that they have become corrupted and possibly confused in the popular mind.

GÁTU RÍMA.

1. Guest goes wandering from the hall,
    Silent and blind is he;
   Meets he with an eldern man
    All with hair so grey.

2. Meets he with an eldern man,
    All with hair so grey;
   "Why art thou so silent, Guest the Blind,
    And wherefore dost thou stray?"

3. "It is not so wonderful
    Though I of speech am slow;
   For riddles have brought me to an evil pass,
    And I lose my head tomorrow.

4. "It is not so wonderful
    Though mournful am I and slow;
   For riddles have brought me to an evil pass,
    And I lose my life tomorrow."

5. "How much of the red, red gold
    Wilt thou give to me,
   If I go in before King Heithrek
    And ask thy riddles for thee?"

6. "Twelve marks of the red, red gold
    Will I give to thee,
   If thou wilt go in before King Heithrek,
    And ransom my head for me."

7. "Go thou into thy courtyard
    And look to thy dwelling, thou,
   While I go in before King Heithrek,
    And ask him riddles now."

8. "Thirty are the riddles
    And one will I propose...
      (*Riddles lost.*)

9. (*First two lines lost.*)
   Thunder is the red drum
    Which beats over all the world."

10. "O hearken now, Heithrek my King,
     Where dost thou know the neighbours,
    Both of whom use the same door,
     And neither one knows the other?"

11. "My thought and thy thought,
     No neighbour is one to other;
    Both of them use the same door,
     Yet neither knows the other."

12. "O hearken now, Heithrek my King,
     Where dost thou know the brothers
    Who roll far away on the outer reefs,
     And have neither fathers nor mothers?"

13. "The Western flow and the Eastern flow,
     Well may they be called brothers;
    They roll far away on the outer reefs
     And have neither fathers nor mothers."

14. "O hearken now, Heithrek my King,
     And what can this be now?—
    Soft as down and hard as horn,
     And white as glistening snow!"

15. "Hear thou this now, Guest the Blind;
     This riddle I understand.—
  The sea it is both soft and hard,
     And flings white spray upon the land."

16. "O hearken now, Heithrek my King,
     Where does the sapling grow,—
  Its root is turned towards high Heaven,
     And its head turned down below?"

17. "The icicle on the high crags,
     No sapling it is I trow,
  Yet its root is turned towards high heaven,
     And its head turned down below."

18. "O hearken now, Heithrek my King,
     Where does that forest grow,—
  It is cut on every holy day,
     And yet there is wood enow?"

19. "The beard which grows on each man's chin,
     No forest is that I trow,
  Though shaved on every holy day,
     And yet there is wood enow."

20. "O hearken now, Heithrek my King,
     Where dost thou know the brothers,—
  Both of them live in the same hall,
     And have neither fathers nor mothers?"

21. "Turf clods and brimstones,
     Neither of the twain are brothers.
  Both of them live in the same hall,
     And have neither fathers nor mothers."

22. "The sow she wanders to her sty,
     She wallows on the green, green earth.
  The boar he grunts and the little pigs squeak,
     And each makes music with his mouth."

23. "O well do I know thy riddle,
     And well it shall be spoke;
  The hammer is raised in every smithy,
     And falls with even stroke."

24. "O well do I know thy riddle,
    Though thereof no boast make I.
  It is Othin who rides upon his steed,
    By land and eke by sea.

25. "O well do I know thy riddle,
    Yet of wisdom I make no display.
  Othin he rides upon his steed
    By night and eke by day."

26. Othin has turned into a wild fowl,
    And flown out from the hall;
  And therein King Heithrek has been burnt,
    He and his nobles all.

27. Othin has turned into a wild fowl,
    And has flown far out to sea;
  He has burnt King Heithrek in his hall,
    And all his company.

INTRODUCTION TO THE SHETLAND
BALLAD OF HILDINA

This ballad has been discussed above, pp. 39 and
164 f. It was taken down by George Low in the
course of a visit made by him to the island of Foula
in the Shetlands in 1774. He was entirely ignorant
of the language, and had apparently no idea as to
the meaning of the actual words, though the general
drift of the ballad was explained to him by the
islander, William Henry, from whom he obtained it
(cf. p. 164). As very few remains of the dialect have
been preserved, apart from the ballad, the interpretation presents great difficulties. The following
translation of the first twelve stanzas is made from
the corrected text given by Dr M. Hægstad in his
edition of the *Hildina* contained in *Skrifter udgivne
af Videnskabsselskabet i Christiania*, 1900 (*Historisk-
Filosofiske Klasse*, 11).

THE SHETLAND BALLAD OF HILDINA

1. It was the Earl from Orkney,
   And counsel of his kin sought he,
   Whether he should the maiden
   Free from her misery.

2. "If thou free the maid from her gleaming hall,
   O kinsman dear of mine,
   Ever while the world shall last
   Thy glory still shall shine."

3. Home came the king,
      Home from the ship's levy
   The lady Hildina she was gone,
      And only her stepmother there found he.

4. "Be he in whatever land,
      This will I prove true,
   He shall be hanged from the highest tree
      That ever upward grew."

5. "If the Earl but come to Orkney,
      Saint Magnus will be his aid,
   And in Orkney ever he will remain—
      Haste after him with speed."

6. The King he stood before his lady,
      And a box on her ear gave he,
   And all adown her lily white cheeks
      The tears did flow truly.

7. The Earl he stood before Hildina,
      And a pat on her cheek gave he,—
   "O which of us two wouldst thou have lie dead,
      Thy father dear or me?"

8. "I would rather see my father doomed,
      And all his company,
   If so my own true lord and I
      May long rule in Orkney.

9. "Now do thou take in hand thy steed,
      And ride thou down to the strand;
   And do thou greet my sire full blithely,
      And gladly will he clasp thy hand."

10. The King he now made answer—
      So sore displeased was he—
   "In payment for my daughter
      What wilt thou give to me."

11. "Thirty marks of the red gold,
      This to thee will I give,
    And never shalt thou lack a son
      As long as I may live."

12. Now long stood the King,
      And long on the Earl gazed he:—
    "O thou art worth a host of sons;
      Thy boon is granted thee."

It will be seen that up to this point, in spite of the loss of the names, there can be little doubt that the subject of the ballad is the story of Hethin and Högni. After this however the narrative deviates from any other known version of this story. It would rather seem that—as in the German Kudrun— two stories, originally distinct, have been brought together in one poem.

NOTES

THE THÁTTR OF NORNAGEST

The Tháttr of Nornagest. A *tháttr* is a portion (episode) of a longer saga, in this case the *Saga of Olaf Tryggvason* which is found in the *Flateyjarbók.*

I. *King Olaf Tryggvason,* one of the most famous kings of Norway (r. 995–1000). He compelled the country to accept Christianity. For accounts of his life and times, see the *Story of Olaf Tryggvison* in the *Heimskringla,* vol. I, pp. 221–378; and also the longer *Saga of King Olaf Tryggwason,* translated by Sephton.

Trondhjem, originally the name, not of a town, but of the entire district round the Trondhjem Fjord.

A man came to him. Cf. the *Saga of Olaf Tryggvason (Heimskringla),* ch. 71.

Guest. Here a pun is intended, the word *Gestr* in Icelandic signifying a 'guest' as well as a 'stranger.'

The Contentious. The word in the text, '*þingbítr,*' seems to mean 'sharp in debate,' and to refer to his ready wit and astuteness in litigation.

Guest said that he had been prime-signed. To 'prime-sign' signified to make the *prima signatio* or sign of the Cross over a person, preliminary to baptism. People so 'prime-signed' were admitted to certain parts of the Mass and to social intercourse in Christian communities. See the *Saga of Egil Skallagrímsson,* ch. 50 ''King Athelstan [of England] was a good Christian....He asked Thorolf and his brother to let themselves be prime-signed; for this was a common practice with both merchants and soldiers who took service under Christians. Men who were prime-signed had free intercourse with both Christians and heathens, and followed whatever religion they liked best. Thorolf and Egil did as the King asked them, and both were prime-signed."

Svein Forkbeard, King of Denmark from 986 (?) to 1014, and of England also during the last year of his life.

The Emperor Otto, i.e. Otto II, 973–983.

Dane-work, i.e. the Danish Wall still partially preserved, which divided Jutland from the land of the Saxons and stretched from near the city of Slesvig to the marsh-land along the River Treene.

King Harold Gormsson appears to have reigned for about fifty years and to have died probably in 986. He was nick-named Harold 'Bluetooth' (or perhaps 'Blacktooth'). About 974 he fought the Emperor Otto II, and Earl Haakon of Norway aided him. Both Harold and Haakon were forced to accept Christianity, but Haakon afterwards renounced it.

Earl Haakon the Heathen, i.e. Earl Haakon the Great, or the Bad, who ruled over Norway, 975–995.

Guthmund. Cf. the *Saga of Hervör and Heithrek*, ch. 1. See also Saxo Grammaticus, *Dan. Hist.*, pp. 346–349, where Guthmund is described as a magician dwelling in the land of the Perms. But see *Glasisvellir*, below.

Glasisvellir. Cf. the *Saga of Hervör and Heithrek*, ch. 1. For the name of the tree or grove called *Glasir* beside Othin's abode in Valhalla, see *Skáldskaparmál*, ch. 34: "Glasir stands with golden foliage before the halls of the God of Victory." See also *Bjarkamál in Forna*, str. 3.

II. *Ulf the Red* was standard-bearer to Olaf Tryggvason at the Battle of Svöld (cf. the *Saga of Olaf Tryggvason, Heimskringla*, ch. 56), where he slew great numbers of the enemy.

The Bay, i.e. Christiania Fjord and the adjacent coasts.

King Half. See *Hálfssaga*, ch. 10; and *Flateyjarbók*, II, pp. 136, 137. King Half had a chosen band of warriors numbering about sixty, who were subject to strict discipline and rules which Professor Craigie (*The Icelandic Sagas*, p. 94) suggests were modelled on those of the Jómsvíkings. For instance, "It was one of their customs always to lie off the ends of promontories. Secondly, they made a rule of never pitching tents on their ships and never clewing up the sail on account of bad weather." The incident referred to in the text is not mentioned in the Saga.

No halls had been built in Norway. The writer probably means to contrast the stone halls of his own day with the wooden structures of earlier times.

The Harping of Gunnar, a lost poem. The legend here referred to is told in *Völsunga Saga*, ch. 37 (and elsewhere), doubtless from an old lay.—'King Attila had Gunnar cast into a pit full of snakes...and his hands were tied. Guthrún sent him a harp, and he was so skilful in harping that he could play it with his toes; and he harped so well that hardly anyone had ever heard such skilful playing, even with the hand. So beautifully did he play that all the snakes were lulled to sleep except one horrible big adder which crept up to him and stung him to the heart. Thus he perished with great courage.'

Gunnar, the son of Gjúki, is the central figure both of the Norse story and of the German *Nibelungenlied*, in which he is called Gunther. In reality, he was overthrown and killed by the Huns in 437, after which the Burgundians moved from the Rhine to the district now known as Burgundy.

The Ancient Wiles of Guthrún. It is generally believed that this is the name of another lost heroic poem. But the title may possibly mean *The Adventures of Guthrún*, in which case the poem referred to may be the well-known *Ancient Lay of Guthrún* (*Guðrúnarkviða hin forna*). This latter poem is alluded to in ch. 9 below under the title of *Guðrúnarræða*.

IV. *The Land of the Franks*, the Rhineland. As far back as the fifth century the Franks occupied that region—to the north of the Burgundians.

Sigurth the son of Sigmund. The story of Sigurth the
Völsung is related in *Völsunga Saga.*

Hundingsbani, i.e. 'Slayer of Hunding.' See *Völsunga
Saga,* ch. 9.

V. *It chanced one day that,* etc. Chapters 5 and 6 are mainly
taken from the poem *Reginsmál* of which strophes 13–26
are quoted in our text. *Reginsmál* is the first poem of a trilogy
dealing with the early adventures of Sigurth. The two remaining poems *Fáfnismál* and *Sigrdrifumál* are used only in
the last two sentences of ch. 6.

Yngvi is a name of the god Frey, from whom the kings of
Norway and the early kings of Sweden were believed to have
sprung.

Fafnisbani, i.e. 'Slayer of Fafnir.' Cf. ch. 6 *infra.* See
also *Völsunga Saga,* ch. 18.

The Imperial Power had not, etc. This may mean either
the refounding of the Western Empire by Charlemagne,
A.D. 800, or possibly the gaining of the Imperial throne by
Otto I, King of the Germans, in 962.

VI. *Sigurth prepared for battle,* etc. An account of this
battle is given in *Völsunga Saga,* ch. 17.

The sea-king's steed. The text has *Ræfils hestum,* lit.
'Ræfil's horses.' Ræfil was a legendary sea-king. The
names of such characters are frequently used in 'kennings'
(i.e. poetic circumlocutions) like this.

Hnikar, a name of the god Othin in the *Grímnismál*
(str. 47) and elsewhere.

The Moon's sister. The text has *systur Mána,* 'Máni's
sister,' i.e. the sun. *Máni,* the old word for the moon, is
preserved in Iceland only in a mythological sense, the ordinary
word in use for moon being *tungl. Máni* and *Sól* (the sun)
were brother and sister. See *Vafþrúþnismál,* str. 23; also
Gylfaginning, ch. 11, 12.

Order their array, lit. 'draw up a wedge-shaped column'
—a favourite battle-formation, the origin of which was
ascribed to Othin.

Stumbling is bad luck, etc. So Wilken (gloss. *s.v. fyrir*, 2.) Vigfússon and Gering transl. 'It is an ill thing to outrun one's luck.'

Friesland. In early times the Frisians occupied a much greater extent of coast than now, reaching from the boundary between Holland and Belgium on one side to beyond the mouth of the Weser on the other—apart from the Frisians inhabiting the west coast of Slesvig.

The 'blood-eagle' was a form of vengeance practised by the heathen Scandinavians in battle when anyone captured the slayer of his father. The ribs were cut in the shape of an eagle, and the lungs torn out through the opening. The Northumbrian King Ella (Ælla) is said to have been put to death in this way by the sons of Ragnar Lothbrók. Cf. the *Saga of Ragnar Loðbrók and his sons*, ch. 18; also the *Tháttr of Ragnar's Sons*, ch. 3.

Hugin and Munin were Othin's attendant ravens who gave him information. See *Grímnismál*, str. 20; *Gylfaginning*, ch. 38; *Ynglingasaga (Heimskringla)*, ch. 7.

The story of Sigurth Fafnisbani. The whole story of the loves of Sigurth and Brynhild is related in the *Völsunga Saga*, ch. 20–32. It is uncertain whether the reference here is to the *Völsunga Saga* as we have it or to an earlier form of the story.

VII. *Gjuki* is mentioned under the form *Gebica* in the *Lex Burgundionum (c.* 500 A.D.). Nothing more is known of him from historical sources; but he is mentioned in *Skáldskaparmál*, ch. 41, *Völsunga Saga* ch. 25, and in the *Edda Poems*, as the father of Gunnar and Guthrún. His name appears also (as *Gifica, Gibicho*, etc.) in the Anglo-Saxon poem *Widsiþ*, the Latin poem *Waltharius*, and in several early German poems.

Sigurth Hring, a legendary king of Sweden and Denmark, and the father of Ragnar Loðbrók. His story is related at length in a fragment of the *Skjöldunga Saga*; and he is probably identical with the *Sigifridus* who is mentioned in several Frankish Chronicles under the year 812 as carrying on hostilities against another Danish King *Anulo*.

The sons of Gandalf were in constant hostility with King Harold the Fairhaired and his father. They owned Alfheimar and Vingulmörk along the Swedish coast of the Kattegat. Cf. the *Story of Halfdan the Black (Heimskringla)*, ch. 1, 4; also the *Story of Harold the Fairhaired (Heimskringla)*, ch. 1 etc.

Gunnar and Högni. The story of the relations of Gunnar and Högni with Sigurth is told in *Völsunga Saga*, ch. 26 f.

Jarnamotha. The locality is unknown. There were large forests in Holstein in the Middle Ages called ' Iarnawith' and ' Isarnho'; cf. Müllenhoff, *Deutsche Altertumskunde*, v, p. 122.

hazlewood poles had been set up, etc. The verb *hasla*, used in the sense of 'to challenge (to a pitched battle),' means, lit. 'to enhazle' a battlefield, i.e. to mark out the space reserved for a pitched battle with hazel poles. Cf. the *Saga of Egil Skallagrímsson*, ch. 52.

The Kurir were the people of Courland (perhaps Lithuanians). The *Kvænir* were the Finnish inhabitants of the northern portion of what is now Sweden. King Alfred, in his translation of *Orosius*, inserts an original account of Norway and the neighbouring regions which was given to him by a Norwegian called Ohthere. It is there stated that beyond the mountains which bound the northern part of Norway was 'the land of the Cwenas.' Cf. also the *Saga of Egil Skallagrímsson*, ch. 14.

Starkath, the ideal warrior of old time in the North. Probably originally a historical figure, he became the centre of much legendary matter, and, as often happened in such cases, he was even credited with the composition of many poems, notably that on the Battle of Brávöll—an event which probably took place long after his time. In Saxo Grammaticus, *Dan. Hist.*, pp. 246–258, he corresponds to the unnamed "Old Warrior" mentioned in *Beowulf*, l. 2041 ff.

Fenhring, in Hörthaland in Norway, not far from Bergen.

Lund, the old ecclesiastical capital of Denmark, situated in Skaane in the extreme south of Sweden. Not only Skaane, but also the neighbouring provinces (Halland, etc.) belonged in early times to Denmark.

VIII. *Starkath had committed a foul murder.* For this story see Saxo Grammaticus, *Dan. Hist.*, p. 314 ff. Saxo says that the rule of King Ali or Ole was so hateful to the Zealanders that twelve of their generals resolved to put him to death, bribing Starkath to join them. Although a personal friend of Ole, Starkath agreed to do so, and murdered him in his bath. He afterwards repented bitterly, "and to atone for his crime slew some of those who had inspired him to it."

Travels. I have followed the reading *ferða*, 'travels,' adopted by Wilken, not *frænda*, as in the *Fornaldar Sögur*, ed. by Ásmundarson. The latter would read: "The King wanted him to tell him much more about the history of his relatives."

IX. *Germans say*, etc. For the German story of the murder of Sigurth see the *Nibelungenlied*, str. 985 ff.

Guthrúnarrætha. This is no doubt the poem commonly called *Guðrúnarkviða hin forna*, the opening of which narrates how Sigurth's horse came home riderless.

Brynhild and the ogress chanted, etc. The following lay is found in the *Edda Poems* under the title of *Helreið Brynhildar* ('The Hell-ride of Brynhild').

From the Land of the Romans, lit. 'From Valland'—the 'land of the Valar,' i.e. the Celts or Romans. Here the reference is doubtless to the Roman territories on the west bank of the Rhine. In the *Nibelungenlied*, Gunther (i.e Gunnar) is represented as reigning at Worms. Cf. p. 232 below.

Assigned me a home, etc. In the *Codex Regius* of the *Edda Poems* this passage runs as follows: "The courageous king had my swan-form and those of my eight sisters carried beneath an oak."

Hjalmgunnar. See *Sigrdrífumál*, the prose following str. 4. "She (i.e. Sigrdrífa) said that two kings were fighting. One was called Hjalmgunnar. He was old at that time, but a very great warrior, and Othin had promised him victory; but the other was called Agnar, the brother of Autha, whom no being would protect. Sigrdrifa (who was a valkyrie) slew Hjalmgunnar in battle, but Othin pierced her with a sleep-producing thorn in punishment for this," etc.

Fafnir was the serpent who guarded the gold hoard on Gnítaheið till Sigurth slew him and carried off the treasure.

All too long, etc. In the *Codex Regius* of the *Edda Poems* this passage runs as follows: "For far too long a time (? for ever) will women and men be born into the world to overwhelming sorrow."

The Sons of Lothbrok. Ragnar Lothbrók was a famous king who flourished about the middle of the ninth century, and who, according to legend, obtained his name ('Shaggy Breeks') from the shaggy trowsers which he wore when he went to attack a serpent. His various exploits are told in the *Saga of Ragnar Lothbrók*, and in the *Tháttr of the Sons of Ragnar*, and also by Saxo Grammaticus, *Dan. Hist*, pp. 368–380, etc. Among his other adventures he is said to have invaded Northumbria, but he was defeated by King Ella (Ælla) and thrown into a snake-pit, where he "died laughing," as we are told in a late poem (*Krakumál* or the 'Death-song of Ragnar Lothbrók'). His death was afterwards avenged by his sons who invaded England in 866. Practically nothing historical is known of Loðbrók himself, though the achievements of his sons, both in the British Isles and on the continent, are of great historical importance.

In the neighbourhood of the Alps. In 856, Björn Ironside, a son of Ragnar Lothbrók, with Hástein his chief lieutenant, invaded France, and during the years 859–862 made expeditions to Spain, Africa, the south of France, and Italy, capturing Pisa, Luna, etc. There can be no doubt that in their invasion of Italy in 860 the real objective was Rome; but for some unknown reason they returned without approaching it. According to Scandinavian tradition, when they entered Luna they were under the impression that it was Rome, and returned satisfied that their aim was accomplished.

Vifilsborg. This place is identified by Wilken with the modern Avenches in the Canton Vaud (Switzerland).

Make their way there, lit. 'pass over (the mountains) thither.'

X. *Eric*, a famous King of Sweden in the time of Harold the Fairhaired, King of Norway, in the latter half of the ninth century. He is frequently referred to in the Sagas and regarded as the typical great Swedish King of the past.

Upsala, i.e. Old Upsala, the ancient capital of the Swedish kingdom, a few miles from the modern city.

King Harold the Fairhaired, said to have been born *c.* 850 and to have succeeded as King of Vestfold *c.* 860. His conquest of Norway was practically completed at the Battle of Hafrsfjörth (*c.* 872). He is said to have retired in 930 and died *c.* 933

King Hlothver, i.e. Louis I, King of the Franks and Emperor, 814–840.

The Saxons inhabited a large part of north-west Germany and Holland; but the name *Saxland* is often used in a wider sense, i.e. the German part of the Empire.

Nornagest, i.e. 'Gest (or guest) of the Norns.' The Norns were represented in Scandinavian mythology as women with the power of shaping human destiny. See *Helgakviða Hundingsbana*, I, str. 2; *Gylfaginning*, chs. 15, 16; Saxo Grammaticus, *Dan. Hist.*, p. 223; the *Saga of Burnt Njál*, ch. 156. Similar beliefs occur in Greek stories about the Fates (Κλῶθες) e.g. the late Greek legend of the birth of Meleager. Cf. p. 13 above.

XII. *Three hundred.* I have used round figures here as elsewhere. Strictly the Norse 100 is 120.

THE THÁTTR OF SÖRLI

I. *Vanakvisl.* The opening sentence may be compared with *Ynglingasaga*, ch. 1, in the *Heimskringla*. From this it appears that Vanakvísl is the River Don, though strictly *kvísl* means the fork (delta) of a river.

Æsir and Vanir, two sets of Scandinavian deities; but the references to the River Don and Asia are due to the learned speculations of later times, suggested partly by the resemblance of *Asia* and *Æsir*. According to *Ynglingasaga*, chs. 1–4, there was war between the Æsir and the Vanir, which was concluded by an exchange of hostages. The Vanir gave to the Æsir three of their leading people—Njörth and his children Frey and Freyja. Othin made Njörth and Frey temple-priests, and Freyja a temple-priestess. What is said about Freyja here is not mentioned in *Ynglingasaga*; but from the poems of the *Edda* it is clear that she was the Aphrodite of northern mythology.

Asgarth. For a description of Asgarth, the home of the Æsir, see *Gylfaginning*, chs. 2, 9, 14, etc.

Men in Asia called Alfregg, etc. For Dvalin, cf. the *Saga of Hervör and Heithrek*, ch. 2 and note.

Lived in a rock; cf. *Völuspá*, str. 48.

Necklace. For the *Brísingamen*, Freyja's treasure, see *Thrymskviða*, str. 12, etc. Cf. also *Beowulf*, l. 1199.

II. *Nál*, i.e. 'Needle.'

Loki. See *Gylfaginning*, ch. 33; and the *Edda Poems*, passim.

So much favoured by the great good fortune of his lord. Cf. *Laxdœla Saga*, ch. 40 'Mun konungr [i.e. Olaf Tryggvason] vera giftudrjúgr ok hamingju-mikill.'

III. *Frithfrothi*, the mythical peace-king of the Danes. See *Skáldskaparmál*, ch. 43. He is often split up into two different characters, as by Saxo Grammaticus. (See especially *Dan. Hist.*, Book v, which gives an account of the great Frothi.)

Erling and Sörli. Their story is told in the *Saga of Sörli the Strong* (*Fornaldar Sögur*, III.).

Skerries of the Elf. Rocky islands near the mouth of the Göta Elv not far from Göteborg.

IV. *Halfdan*, surnamed Brönufóstri. See the *Saga of Sörli the Strong*, ch. 11, where he is represented as King of Sweden.

Roeskilde, the old capital of Sjælland, now the ecclesiastical capital of Denmark.

Ellithi. See the *Saga of Thorstein Víkingson* (passim), and the *Saga of Friðjóf the Bold* (passim).

Gnoth. The ship Gnoth belonged to Ásmund, who was called after it 'Gnoðar-Ásmund.' Cf. the *Saga of Egil and Asmund*, ch. 17; and the *Saga of Grím Loðinkinni*, ch. 3. See also the *Saga of Hromund Greipsson*, ch. 1.

Long Serpent, i.e. the warship of Olaf Tryggvason.

As is told in the poem, etc. The poem is now lost.

The poem of which he is the subject. The Saga here quotes a difficult and obscure stanza which I have omitted.

Högni...went raiding in the Baltic, etc. In *Widsið*, l. 21, Högni is said to have ruled the *Holmryge*, i.e., no doubt, the Rugii on the coast of Pomerania.

V. *Hjarrandi* is the name of Hethin's father in all the Norse forms of the story; but originally this would seem to have been the name of Hethin's minstrel—the *Hôrant* of *Kudrun*, and the *Heorrenda* of *Deor*.

Serkland, i.e. Africa, 'Saracen Land.' It is only in this story that Hethin is said to come from here. Saxo Grammaticus calls him a Norwegian. Cf. also *Widsiþ*, l. 21, which gives the name of an unknown people.

Göndul, the name of one of the Valkyries. See *Völuspá*, str. 31; *Hákonarmál*, passim; *Skáldskaparmál*, chs. 2 and 47.

VI. *Heithrek Ulfham.* For Heithrek Ulfham see the *Saga of Hervör and Heithrek*, ch. 16.

VII. *She asked him.* I have followed Rafn's text. The Reykjavík ed. apparently has a misprint here—*hann* for *hón*.

He thrust the Queen down in front of the prow, etc. The murder of the Queen is peculiar to this saga.

VIII. *This harrowing torment continued*, etc. A good deal has been written on the subject of the Unending Battle, which many writers believe to have been of mythological origin. Very often, however, it appears in local traditions. See Frazer's *Pausanias*, vol. II, p. 443 (the reference to the Battle of Marathon), where a considerable number of parallels are given. See also Panzer, *Hilde-Gudrun*, p. 328. Cf. p. 43, note 1 above.

Olaf Tryggvason. See the *Tháttr of Nornagest*, ch. 1 and note.

IX. *Jarnskjöld.* Cf. *Fornmanna Sögur*, vol. III, p. 125 ff. (*Saga of Olaf Tryggvason*).

Glance of his eye, etc. Literally, "He has the *ægishjálmr*." This is a poetical expression for a glance inspiring terror.

THE SAGA OF HROMUND GREIPSSON

I. *Gnothar-Asmund*, i.e. Asmund of the Gnoth, who was so called from his ship 'Gnoth' (cf. p. 230 above). For an account of him see the *Saga of Egil and Asmund* (in *Fornaldar Sögur*, vol. III), especially ch. 17. He is mentioned also in the *Saga of Grím Loðinkinni*, ch. 2. A different account of Olaf's family is given in *Göngu-Hrólfs Saga*, ch. 38.

Garthar in Denmark. The geography of the story is by no means clear. Elsewhere in this saga Olaf's realm would seem to be situated in Sweden, while references in other works, e.g. *Landnámabók*, I, ch. 3, *Hversu Noregr Bygthist*, ch. 2 (*Fornaldar Sögur*, II, p. 7) etc., point to Norway, especially the provinces of Thelamörk and Hörthaland, as the home of Hromund and his family.

Hromund. According to *Landnámabók*, I, ch. 3, Ingolf and Leif, the first settlers in Iceland (A.D. 874) were the great grandsons of Hromund Greipsson. This would seem to show that he lived in the second half of the eighth century. See also the *Saga of Halfdan Eysteinsson*, ch. 1.

Bild and Voli. For these names, see Introduction to this saga, p. 59, and the note to *Mistletoe* below.

Ulfasker. A corruption of *Elfasker*. Cf. *Gríplur*, str. 25, and note to *Skerries of the Elf*, p. 229 above.

Dragon, a common term for a large type of warship in the Viking Age.

Scoundrels. The text has *Blámenn,* i.e. lit. 'Black men,' negroes. But in the Romantic Sagas, owing probably to the influence of stories relating to the Saracens, pirates are described as *Blámenn,* even in stories relating exclusively to the North. Cf. *The Ballad of Hjálmar and Angantyr* (refrain), p 184, above.

II. *I am going to be Othin's guest,* is a euphemism for 'be slain,' and is equivalent to 'go to Valhalla,' the abode of slain warriors which belonged to Othin. See the *Saga of Egil Skallagrímsson,* ch. 81, where Thorgerth, Egil's daughter, says that she will have no supper till she "sup with Freyja."

No blade would wound Hröngvith. It is not uncommon to hear that a warrior, usually an unsympathetic character, was immune through spells from wounds inflicted by weapons; cf. *Beowulf,* l. 804, where this is stated of Grendel.

III. *Hebrides.* The word *Suthreyjar,* here translated Hebrides, properly means all the islands off the west coast of Scotland. The modern form of the word is *Sodor,* surviving in the name of the diocese of 'Sodor and Man.'

Ghosts. It will be seen from the context that the word *draugr* here translated 'ghost,' is in reality the animated corpse of the dead man. This is a common feature of Norse stories (e.g. the *Saga of Grettir the Strong,* ch. 18).

IV. *Valland,* i.e. France, lit. the 'Land of the *Valar,*' i.e. of the Celts or Romans. In Anglo-Saxon literature the French are sometimes called *Galwalas,* i.e. the 'Walas (Welsh) of Gaul.' See also the *Tháttr of Nornagest,* ch. 9 and note.

And he added, etc. Are we to assume a lacuna here? The composition of this saga is however far from perfect. In certain passages (e.g. at the beginning of this chapter) one is inclined to suspect that someone has tried to combine two different texts of the story.

Finger nails, etc. Cf. the physiological fact of the growth of the finger nails after death, and the legend of Charlemagne according to which his beard grew through a stone table after his death.

Gunnlöth. Other documents appear to make Hromund a Norwegian, and this is what we should gather from *Landnámabók* quoted above (p. 231, note). See *Hversu Noregr Bygðist,* ch. 2.

Mistletoe, the name of the sword again connects this story with that of Balder who is stated in *Völuspá,* str. 32 and *Gylfaginning,* ch. 49 to have been killed by a piece of mistletoe.

V. *Dagny,* the wife of Ingjóld, who was the friend of Grím Lothinkinni. See the *Saga of Grím Loðinkinni,* ch. 3.

Hálogaland. See *Hervarar Saga,* ch. 1 and note; and also the Sagas of *Ketil Hæng* and *Grím Loðinkinni.*

Voli and Bild, etc. At this point the writer of the saga has omitted part of the dialogue in which Olaf threatens to hang Hromund. Cf. *Gríplur,* p. 383, str. 20, 21.

VI. *Helgi* is known elsewhere as Helgi Haddingjaskati, e.g. in the short text called *Hversu Noregr Bygðist,* ch. 2 (*Fornaldar Sögur,* II, p. 7). According to the prose at the end of *Helgakviða Hundingsbana* II, Helgi Haddingjaskati and Kara were reincarnations of Helgi Hundingsbani and Sigrún, the hero and heroine of this poem. Their story was given in a poem called *Káruljóð* which is now lost. See however Vigfússon and Powell, *Corpus Poeticum Boreale,* vol. I, pp. 129 and 130.

On the frozen surface of Lake Vener. This story is perhaps taken from that of the battle related in *Skáldskaparmál,* ch. 43 and *Ynglingasaga,* ch. 33. Cf. *Beowulf,* l. 2392 ff.

Kara,. For the form *Lara* which appears in the printed editions see p. 62, note, above. In the prose at the end of *Helgakviða Hundingsbana* II, Kara is called a valkyrie.

VIII. *Hagal.* The story of Hagal and Blind is given also at the beginning of *Helgakviða Hundingsbana* II; but here the person disguised as a grinding-maid is Helgi, the hero of the poem.

X. *Who was also called Bavis*; cf. *Helgakv. Hund.* II, str. 2, where he is called *Blindr enn bölvísi* ('skilled in harmful doings')

SAGA OF HERVÖR AND HEITHREK

1. *Finnmark*, i.e. the northernmost part of the Scandinavian Peninsula.

Jötunheimar, i.e. the homes of the *jötnar* or giants. This name occurs frequently in Norse stories, though it is not elsewhere connected with Finnmark.

Ymisland, i.e. the land of *Ýmir*; see below.

Halogaland, i.e. the northern part of Norway stretching from about lat. 65° as far as Finnmark.

Guthmund. Cf. the *Tháttr of Nornagest*, ch. 1 and note.

Glasisvellir. Cf. the *Tháttr of Nornagest*, ch. 1, and note.

Fields of immortality, i.e. lit. 'Fields of the not dead' (*ódainsakr*). Cf. the *Saga of Eiríkr Víðförla*, ch. 1, and the *Saga of Hálfdan Eysteinsson*, ch. 1. See also Saxo Grammaticus, *Dan. Hist.*, p. 129.

Höfund. The name means lit. 'Judge.'

Ymir, i.e. the old 'Rime-giant,' the first being created out of Chaos, from whom the giants sprang; cf. *Völuspá*, str. 3; *Vafþrúþnismál*, str. 21; *Grímnismál*, str. 40; *Hyndluljóð*, str. 33; *Gylfaginning*, chs. 5–8.

Starkath Áludreng. See *Gautreks Saga*, ch. 3, according to which this Starkath is the grandfather of his more famous namesake, for whom see the *Tháttr of Nornagest*, ch. 7 and note. See also Saxo Grammaticus, *Dan. Hist.*, pp. 224, 225.

Elivagar. See *Vafþrúþnismál*, str. 31; *Gylfaginning*, ch. 5; *Hymiskviða*, str. 5.

Alfheimar, a name given to the region between the Gøtaelv and the River Glommen, in the south-east of Norway (now mainly in Sweden). The royal family of this region is frequently mentioned in the history of Harold the Fairhaired and his father, and also in the stories of Sigurth Hring. See the *Tháttr of Nornagest*, ch. 7 and note.

Ey-grim Bolm, i.e. 'Grim of the Island of Bolm.'

Arngrim. See Saxo Grammaticus, *Dan. Hist.*, p. 203 ff.

Berserk. See *Ynglingasaga*, ch. 6.

II. *Dwarfs.* Cf. the story of Svegðir in *Ynglingasaga*, ch. 15.

Dvalin is the name of a dwarf in *Völuspá*, str. 11, 14; *Hávamál*, str. 143, and in other of the *Edda* poems. It is, in fact, the typical name for a dwarf. Cf. also *Gylfaginning*, ch. 14, and *Skáldskaparmál*, ch. 3, 57. *Dulin* does not occur elsewhere, though *Durin* is found in *Völuspá*, str. 10.

Standing in the doorway of the stone, etc. Cf. *Völuspá*, str. 48.

Your sword, etc. Cf. *Skáldskaparmál*, ch. 49. "Now I have drawn *Dáinsleif*, which the dwarfs made and which must cause a man's death every time it is drawn, and never fails in its stroke."

Tyrfing. It has been suggested that this name is derived from *tyrfi*, 'resinous fir-tree,' owing to its flaming like resinous fir-wood. In early times it was customary for swords to be called by names ending in *-ing*. Cf. the swords *Hrunting* in *Beowulf*, l. 1457, etc., *Nægling*, *ibid.*, l. 2680, and *Mimming* in *Waldhere*, l. 3, etc., etc.

Perms. The text has *um Bjarmaland* ('in the land of the Bjarmar,' i.e. the *Beormas* of Ohthere's Voyage in Alfred's translation of *Orosius*. It is generally reached, not as here, apparently, by the Baltic, but by voyages round the North Cape. The name is generally supposed to be connected with *Perm*, and in early times may have comprehended the Zyrianians, as well as the Permians proper and the Votiaks. There is some evidence from place-names that this group of languages was once spoken as far west as the White Sea. Cf. Abercromby, *The Pre- and Proto-historic Finns*, p. 10 f.

Svafrlami. The text (H) followed by the Reykjavik edition here has Sigrlami—which can hardly be right. Rafn's ed. reads Svafrlami.

Twelve sons. For Arngrim's Sons, Cf. *Hyndluljóth*, str. 23, 24; Saxo Grammaticus, *Dan. Hist.*, pp. 203–205; *Saga of Örvar Odd*, ch. 14.

Twins. See the *Saga of Harold the Fairhaired (Heimskringla),* ch. 18, where again we find twins both receiving the same name.

Mistletoe. A sword of the same name occurs in the *Saga of Hromund Greipsson* (see above).

Hrotti. Cf. *Hrunting,* the sword of Hunferth in *Beowulf,* l. 1457 etc. See also the note to *Tyrfing,* p. 235.

III. *Yule,* a festival of heathen times, approximately at Christmas, but rather later.

Feast, lit. 'At the Bragi-cup.' The custom of making vows in connection with these toasts was carried on into Christian times, an interesting example being found in the *Saga of Olaf Tryggvason (Heimskringla),* ch. 39. See also the *Saga of Haakon the Good (Heimskringla),* ch. 16; and *Helgakviða Hjörvarðssónar,* str. 32.

Angantyr made a vow. In the Royal MS. (see p. 79) it is Hjörvarth who makes the vow and subsequently claims the bride.

Yngvi is the family name of the early Swedish kings. Collectively the early Swedish royal family were called *Ynglingar.* Cf. *Ynglingasaga,* ch. 20.

Never did he, etc. Compare what is said of Högni's sword in *Skáldskaparmál,* ch. 49.

Samsø. The fight at Samsø is described in another MS. of this saga (which is translated in the appendix to Part I, p. 145 ff. above and which contains also the *Death-song of Hjalmar*), as well as in the *Saga of Örvar Odd,* ch. 14, and in Saxo Grammaticus, *Dan. Hist.,* p. 205. The Island of Samsø is situated half way between Jutland and Sjælland.

IV. *Exposing the child,* etc. For the custom of exposing infants, especially girls, at birth, so as to cause their death, see the *Saga of Gunnlaug Ormstungu,* ch. 3, the *Saga of Finnbogi Rammi,* etc. A similar custom prevailed in Ancient Greece. Cf. Plato, *Rep.* v, 461; Aristophanes, *Clouds,* l. 530 f.

Sprinkled with water. Sprinkling a child with water when a name was given to it appears to have been customary in heathen times. Cf. the *Saga of Harold the Fairhaired* (*Heimskringla*), ch. 40; the *Saga of Haakon the Good*, ch. 12; the *Saga of Egil Skallagrimsson*, ch. 31; *Völsunga Saga*, ch. 13.

She grew up, etc. Cf. the description of the later Hervör in ch. 10.

Here is a poem, etc. The poem is probably earlier than the Saga in its present form. Heusler (*Eddica Minora*, p. xxi) refers it to the early part of the twelfth century.

I will give you my necklace, etc. Note the discrepancy between the poem and the prose at this point. In the former it would seem to be Hervör who offers a necklace, and this is what we should expect.

Foolish is he who comes here alone, etc. Cf. J. M. Synge, *The Aran Islands*, III: "We went up on the dun, where Michael said he had never been before after nightfall, though he lives within a stone's throw....These people make no distinction between the natural and the supernatural."

V. *Ghosts*, i.e. the animated corpses of the people buried there.

Nor other kinsman. There is a lacuna in the text of the MS. at this point.

VI. *Bring up the child*, etc. It was customary for men in high station to send their children to be brought up and educated in the houses of relatives and friends.

Reithgotaland is here explained as Jutland; but in ch. 9, Heithrek's subjects are described as *Gotar*, i.e. Goths; and in the latter part of the Saga, from ch. 12 onwards, the subject is clearly a war between the Goths and Huns. The earliest occurrence of the word (in the Swedish Inscription of Rök; cf. also *Vafþrúþnismál*, str. 12) gives not *Reithgotaland*, but *Hraithgotaland*, which suggests that the name may be connected in some way with *Hrethgotan*, a name applied to the Goths in Anglo-Saxon poetry.

VII. *Divination.* The phrase means literally, 'The casting of bits of wood at the sacrifice.' Cf. Tacitus, *Germania*, ch. 10.

Every second man. annanhvárn, apparently for *annanhvern*.

Hall of the Dís. It is not clear who the *dís* was, as the word is used rather loosely for supernatural female beings. Another reference to the *Hall of the Dís* occurs in *Ynglingasaga*, ch. 33. One of the goddesses (Freyja?) may be meant; or it may be the guardian spirit of the family.

VIII. *Land of the Saxons.* Cf. the *Tháttr of Nornagest*, ch. 10 and note.

Sifka and Hlöth. The names here mentioned, together with *Heithrek* and *Angantyr*, are believed by some scholars to recur in *Widsiþ*, l. 116, where we find

Heaðoric and Sifecan, Hliðe and Incgenðeow,

mentioned as being among the followers of Eormenric. These names clearly come from Gothic tradition, but the passage would seem to suggest that *Sifeca* was a man, the Sibich of the German poems. Cf. Chambers, *Widsith*, p. 32. For the name Lotherus in Saxo, see note to ch. 12, p. 242.

Holmgarth, i.e. Novgorod.

IX. *Wendland*, i.e. the 'Land of the Slavs' (Anglo-Saxon *Weonodland*). After the expansion of the Slavs, from the fifth century onwards, this term came to denote an enormous expanse of country, including the coast of Eastern Germany, to which it is applied in the account of the voyage of Wulfstan in Alfred's translation of *Orosius*. In earlier times, when the Goths still occupied Poland and Galicia, the Slavs were restricted to the regions east of these countries.

His horse fell dead. Here the point of the story seems to be missed, or at least not clearly expressed. According to Höfund's fifth maxim (see ch. 6), Heithrek was not to ride his best horse when he was in a hurry.

X. *They had a daughter.* From our text it would appear that Hervör was the daughter of Sifka; but the end of ch. 9 is probably a late addition to the text. In the text printed by Rafn, Hervör is expressly stated to be a daughter of Hergerth.

Ormar is presumably to be identified with the *Wyrmhere* mentioned in *Widsiþ*, l. 119, in connection with the war waged by the Goths against the Huns in defence of their ancient fatherland, round the forest of the Vistula.

Gestumblindi. For this curious name, cf. the *Gestiblindus Gothorum rex* mentioned by Saxo Grammaticus, *Dan. Hist.*, p. 198 ff.

In the King's retinue there were seven men, etc. In the text (*a*) of this saga printed in Rafn's edition (*Fornaldar Sögur*, I, p. 462), there are said to be twelve men here. This is no doubt the right figure, twelve being the regular number in the judicial councils of the North, whether historical or legendary. Thus, e.g. in the *Saga of Olaf the Holy (Heimskringla)*, ch. 96 we read of a council of twelve sages (*spekingar*), whose duty it was to advise the Swedish king, especially in the administration of justice. Similar councils existed in the Danish settlements in England. Thus Lincoln and Stamford had each a council of twelve (cf. Stubbs, *Const. Hist.*, I, p. 106, and n. 4). We may compare the twelve priests who officiated in the sacrifices at Mæren (cf. the *Saga of Olaf the Holy*, *Heimskr.* ch. 115), and the story of the twelve gods who were appointed by Othin as temple priests (*hof-goðar*) to keep up the sacrifices and administer justice among men; cf. *Ynglingasaga*, ch. 2 (*Hyndluljóð*, str. 30; *Gautrekssaga*, ch. 7). In the Irish *Lay of Magnus Barelegs*, the Norwegians are referred to as *Clann an dá comhairleac déag* ('children or clan of the twelve councillors'). Cf. *Laoid Magnius Moir* (*Reliques of Irish Poetry*, by Charlotte Brooke, Dublin 1789, p. 274).

King Heithrek worshipped Frey. One text quoted by Rafn (*Verelius*) has *Freyja* for *Frey.* The boar appears in stories relating to both these deities, e.g. *Gylfaginning*, ch. 49; *Skáldskaparmál*, ch. 35; *Hyndluljóð*, str. 5, 7.

XI. *I wou d that I had that*, etc. On these riddles see Heusler, *Eddica Minora*, p. xc ff.; 'Die altnordischen Rätsel' in *Zeitschrift des Vereins für Volkskunde*, XI, p. 117 ff.; Tupper, *Modern Language Notes*, 18, p. 103; *The Riddles of the Exeter Book*, p. lii, etc. In the original the riddles are all in verse, while the King's answers, except the refrain with which they begin ("Your riddle is a good one," etc.) are in prose.

You went over a bridge, etc. The metrical text given by Rafn (*Fornaldar Sögur*, I, p. 466), has: "A bird flew above thee, a fish swam beneath thee, thou did'st go over a bridge." The prose text given on the same page has: "Thou did'st go over a bridge, and the course of the river was beneath thee, but birds were flying over thy head and on both sides of thee, and that was their road."

Delling's doorway. Delling (perhaps from an obsolete word *dallr*, 'bright, shining') is mentioned in *Vafþrúþnismál*, str. 25, as the 'father of Day.' Possibly he may originally have been a personification of day itself. The expression "before Delling's doorway" occurs also in *Hávamál*, str. 160, where it has been thought to mean 'at sunrise.' See also the genealogy in *Hversu Noregr Bygðist*, ch. 1 (*Fornaldar Sögur*, II, p. 6), where a certain Svanhild is said to be the daughter of Day, the son of Delling, and of Sól (i.e. the sun), the daughter of Mundilfari (cf. *Gylfaginning*, ch. 11).

Wolves are always struggling for it. See *Gylfaginning*, ch. 12 (from *Grímnismál*, str. 39).

He who made it, etc. I have followed Heusler's reading and read *er* for *ker* and *þó* or *sjá* for *þá*.

Laying their eggs. For *verja* read *verpa*.

Have no husbands. For *eigu*, read *eigut*, as on p. 121.

Game of chess. The text has *hneftafl*, i.e. a game having certain features in common with chess which was played in Iceland till the introduction of the latter, probably in the thirteenth century. Game-pieces have been discovered in Iceland which were probably used for this game. Some are plain and hemispherical in shape, others are shaped with a man's head or a dog's head. For a full and interesting description of *hneftafl* see H. J. R. Murray, *A History of Chess*, Oxford, 1913, Appendix I, 'Chess in Iceland,' pp. 443–446.

Ægis meyjar. Ægir or Hlér, the husband of Rann, is a personification of the sea; but the kennings 'Ægir's daughters,' 'Ægir's steed,' etc. for 'billows' are common in poetry. See *Helgakviða Hundingsbana* II, str. 29, and *Bragar-ræður*, ch. 55 (included in Brodeur's translation of the *Prose Edda* as *Skáldskaparmál*, ch. 1).

Reefs. For *brimserkum*, read *brimskerjum*.

Ocean-path. For *brim-reiðar*, read *brim-leiðar*. The passage is possibly corrupt.

That is the hunn. This stanza is difficult to interpret as we have no clear information as to the character of the game. It would seem that like the game of the Welsh *tawlbwrdd*, it was played between sides composed, the one of sixteen 'fair' (white) men, the other of a King (called *hnefa* or *hunn*) and eight 'dark' (black) men. Cf. note to *Game of Chess* above. See also Murray, *A History of Chess*, Oxford 1913, Appendix I, 'Chess in Iceland,' pp. 443–446.

Four walking, etc. This riddle is found in a form almost identical with our text in Jakobsen's *Dialect and Place Names of Shetland* (Lerwick, 1897), p. 53. The 'sow' is also found in the *Exeter Book*, while 'the waves,' 'the anchor' and 'hailstones' have certain affinities with the AS. riddles.

King Itrek's Game. The reference here seems to be to a game something like chess. The text (R) given by Heusler in his edition of the *Eddica Minora*, p. 118, reads: "That is Itrek and Andath when they sit at their game."

Dead men, etc. In this strophe there seems to be an elaborate play on words. The phrase 'dead men' (*dauðar menn*) seems to be a disguise for *val* which means 'the slain' as well as 'hawk.' So also 'channel of blood' seems to be a disguise for *æði* which means 'vein' as well as 'eider-duck.'

Sleipnir. Othin's eight-footed horse. Cf. especially *Gylfaginning*, ch. 42.

Tell me lastly, etc. In *Vafþrúþnismál*, str. 54, Othin makes himself known to Vafþrúþnir by the same question.

XII. *This pike*, etc. This verse is generally supposed to come from a lost poem on Heithrek.

Mountains of Harvathi. It is thought that *Harvathi* may be the early Teutonic name for the Carpathians—a reminiscence of Gothic times.

Humli and Hlöth. These names may be compared with *Humblus* and *Lotherus*, two sons of Dan, the first kings mentioned in Saxo Grammaticus, *Dan. Hist.*, p. 1. For the name *Hlöð* cf. also note to ch. 7, p. 238.

Poem. For this poem on the battle between the Goths and the Huns, see Heusler, *Eddica Minora*, p. vii ff., and notes. In part at least it appears to be very old.

Myrkvith. The forest *Myrkvith* is mentioned also in *Atlakviða*, str. 3, 5, and 13; and in *Helgakviða Hundingsbana*, I, str. 53.

Pillar, lit. 'stone.' I do not know what is meant. Possibly *Guðrúnarkviða* III, str. 3 may be compared.

Danaper's Shore. *Danpr* is treated as a personal name in *Rígsþula*, str. 49, but it is more likely to have been originally the name of the River Dnieper (mentioned by Jordanes, *The Origins and Deeds of the Goths*, ch. 5, 52, as *Danaper*), which was within the territories of the Goths in the fourth century.

XIII. *Gizur.* There appear to be reminiscences of this story in Saxo, Book V, e.g. in regard to the numbering of the Hunnish forces. *Gizur* seems to correspond to Eric in Saxo p. 190 f. It has been suggested that he is Othin in disguise.

Hazle stakes. Cf. the *Tháttr of Nornagest*, ch. 7 (note).

XIV. *They rode forthwith...against the Huns.* It has been suggested by Heinzel that this battle between the Goths and the Huns was the great battle fought on the Catalaunian Plain in 451 A.D.; but the passage in *Widsið* cited on p. 238 points rather to Poland.

Drew...lips, lit. 'drew back his moustache.'

Dunheith and the other place names are unknown.

XV. *The Goths were defending*, etc. Cf. *Widsiþ*, l. 121 ff.

XVI. *Ivar Vithfathmi*. For Ivar Vithfathmi and his family, see *Ynglingasaga*, chs. 44, 45, and the first fragment of *Skjöldunga Saga* (printed in the *Fornaldar Sögur*, i, p. 285 ff.), chs. 1–3.

Harold Hilditönn. The fullest account of Harold Hilditönn is that given by Saxo Grammaticus, *Dan. Hist.*, p. 296 ff. See also the fragments of the *Skjöldunga Saga*, ch. 4 ff.

Gautland, i.e. the Land of the *Geatas* in *Beowulf*, the modern Götaland (whether Vestergötland or Östergötland or both), comprising roughly speaking the southern portions of Sweden, exclusive of the Danish districts (Skaane etc).

Harold of the Red Moustache. He was King of Agthir. A daughter of his, also called Ása, was married to Guthröth, King of Vestfold—the *Godefridus* who fought against Charlemagne and died in 810. See *Ynglingasaga*, ch. 53. Their son was Hálfdan the Black, the father of Harold the Fairhaired.

Sigurth Hring. See the *Tháttr of Nornagest*, ch. 7 and note.

Battle of Brávöll. The chief accounts of this battle are to be found in the second fragment of the *Skjöldunga Saga*, ch. 8 f. (see above); and in Saxo Grammaticus, *Dan. Hist.*, pp. 309 ff.

The Sons of King Ragnar. For Ragnar Lothbrók and his sons, see the *Tháttr of Nornagest*, ch. 9 and note.

A sea-king. Cf. the *Saga of Olaf the Holy (Heimskringla)*, ch. 4.

The Sons of Eric Björnson were Önund and Björn. These are probably to be identified with the Swedish kings Bern and Anoundus mentioned in Rembertus' *Life of St Ansgar*, chs. 11 and 19, in connection with the saint's missionary visits to Sweden (*c.* 830).

Bragi Skald was the great grandfather of Arinbjörn the friend of Egil Skallagrímsson. In the *Saga of Egil Skalla-*

grímsson, ch. 59, he is said to have saved his life by composing in one night a poem in honour of King Björn. Some fragments of his poems have been preserved—the earliest datable Norse poems which have come down to us.

King Harold the Fairhaired. See the *Tháttr of Nornagest*, ch. 10, and note.

Eric the Victorious. The battle won by Eric the Victorious over Styrbjörn at Fyrisvellir seems to have taken place between 980 and 985. Several Runic inscriptions contain references to it. The statement that Harold the Fairhaired died in Eric's time can hardly be correct; for Harold is believed to have died in 933.

Fyrisvellir, on the banks of the Fyrisá, close to the site of the modern town of Upsala.

Olaf the Swede. The traditional date of his conversion is 1008.

Olaf the Saint, ex-King of Norway, whence he had been expelled in 1028, was killed at the Battle of Stiklestad in 1030 in an attempt to recover the throne.

He tried to put an end to, etc. An interesting account of the heathen ceremonies of the Swedes, dating from shortly after the middle of the eleventh century, is given by Adam of Bremen in his *History of the Church of Hamburg*, Book IV., ch. 26 f.

The sacred tree. The sacrificial tree in question is presumably that mentioned in schol. 134 to Adam of Bremen as standing beside the great temple of Upsala.

Eymund, c. 1050–*c.* 1060.

Steinkel, 1060–1066.

Haakon the Red, 1066–1079?

Ingi I, d. *c.* 1110. He, Hallstein and Blótsvein were all reigning in 1081.

Philippus, d. 1118.

Ingi II, d. 1125.

GRIPLUR I

10. *Gnoth-Ásmund*, etc. For notes on people mentioned in the *Griplur*, see notes to the *Saga of Hromund Greipsson*, p. 231 ff. above.

13. *Draupnir's beautiful blood*, a *kenning* for 'gold rings.' Draupnir was the name of Othin's ring which was made by the smith Eitri and sent to Othin by his brother Brokk. Its special value lay in the fact that every ninth night, eight gold rings dropped from it. Cf. *Skáldskaparmál*, ch. 35. Cf. also *Völuspá*, str. 15, where Draupnir is mentioned in the list of dwarfs.

THE FAROESE BALLAD OF NORNAGEST

Refrain. According to Lyngbye the refrain should be:
> *You dare not give counsel in trouble*, etc.

Others have it
> *Let them have help in trouble.*

Schrøter took down the first two verses as follows:
> A ballad there is of Nornagest,—
>> *You dare not give counsel in trouble*—
> In manly virtues among the best.—
>> *Let every lad do so!*
> Twelve oxen were led to the Market Square,
> And onward thence to a castle fair.—
>> *Grani bore gold from the heath.*

> The King he thought to hew them to earth,—
>> *You dare not give counsel in trouble*—
> With courage and joy does he sally forth,—
>> *Let every lad do so!*
> The King he struck such a mighty blow,
> That the blood from the wounds did swiftly flow.
>> *Grani bore gold from the heath.*

10. *The mightiest champion*, etc. In Lyngbye's version 10 and 11 are transposed. Hammershaimb's is no doubt the correct order.

15. *Was Högni*, etc. Lyngbye here inserts a stanza:

> Högni was a mighty man:
> Swarthy of hue was he as I ween.

16. *Rich, brave*, etc. The Suderø version of the ballad here substitutes at the beginning of the line: "They were old and grey."

31. *The saddle-buckle*, etc. In Lyngbye's version of the *Ballad of Regin the Smith*, v. 131 (omitted by Hammershaimb) the following stanza is found:

> [Grani] sprang across the pool
> And his saddle-buckle brake.
> And as I ween that saddle-buckle
> Nornagest did take.

In the *Ballad of Regin the Smith* we are told that the accident to Grani occurred when Sigurth was on his way home from Gnítaheið after slaying Fafnir. Grani was heavily laden with treasure and Sigurth also was mounted on him, so that the accident there appears perfectly natural.

In days, etc. So Hammershaimb. Lyngbye has:

> In days gone by full far have I strayed
> In search of my candle and span of days.

In the land. Here Lyngbye has:

> In the Land of the Franks is a lake broad and wide:
> O there does my span of life abide.
>
> O there does my span of life abide:
> And so for long I have wandered far and wide."

But he adds a version corresponding to Hammershaimb's in a footnote and states that it is frequently sung so.

42. *The courteous man.* According to Lyngbye, by a 'courteous man,' the Faroese mean a *Scotsman* and says that

the origin of the word (*kurtis*) is unknown. It is of course the same as the Icelandic *kurteis* which is a French loan-word.

According to Lyngbye it was still part of popular Faroese legend in his day that Nornagest kept his candle in a little leaden casket which was sunk in a lake. Lyngbye says that Nornagest was regarded as the 'Nestor' of the Faroes, which is quite in accordance both with his "three hundred years" mentioned in the saga, and with the unusually long span of life often associated with the External Soul of folklore.

THE BALLAD OF HJALMAR AND ANGANTYR

1. *In a high oak-tree.* In the version of this ballad obtained by Hammershaimb at Sumbø the first line runs 'A man there lived on (lit. 'in') an island high,' whereas in the *Ballad of Arngrim's Sons,* v. 3, we are told that Arngrim and his sons lived 'under' an oak. Possibly the first line of our text is a confusion of these two versions. The error is made more comprehensible by the fact that there are no trees on the Faroes, and so the phrase must have been a meaningless jingle of words to the singers.

Arngrim's sons from Africa. The text has 'Arngrim's sons from Bláland,' by which the Faroese ballads and the *Fornaldar Sögur* generally mean Africa. Here, however, we should more naturally have expected 'Norway,' and it is very probable that, as Hammershaimb suggests, we here have the refrain in a corrupt form as so often happens. Probably 'from Bláland' (*af Blálandum*) should be 'from Bólmland' (*af Bólmlandi*), i.e. from the Island of Bólm, but the Faroese may have substituted the more familiar name for that of the island with which they were unacquainted.

2. *The champions Hjalmar,* etc. The Sumbø version has:

He has eleven sons so dear;
The twelfth is the warrior Angantyr,

and also inserts immediately following a verse giving reasons
for the voyage:

> News then came to Angantyr
> That a man there was had a daughter fair.

4. *They hoisted their sail*, etc. Cf. *Sigmundar Kvæði*,
str. 13, 28, 48.

5. *Their anchor they cast*, etc. Cf. *Magna Dans (Icelandic
Fornkvæði)* v. 3, with which this is practically identical.

6. *Angantyr eagerly*, etc. The lit. transl. of the text is 'Angantyr was the first to step,' etc.; but the following v. has
'Hjalmar was the first to step!' The Sumbø version, which
is undoubtedly better here, has

> *Angantyr loypur so tungliga á land*
> Angantyr leapt so heavily to land,

instead of

> *Fyrstur steig Angantýr fótum á land*
> Angantyr was the first to step with his feet to land.

10. *Here sittest thou*, etc. In the Sumbø version, Hjalmar's
request is not recorded. The repetition of Angantyr's request
in our text, if it has any significance at all, implies that both
Hjalmar and Angantyr made the proposal.

18. *O franklin, lend me*, etc. The Sumbø version here
inserts an additional verse.

> Angantyr is so vile a troll,
> So are his kinsfolk and followers all.

19. *Forth of the hall*. In the Sumbø version the fight took
place outside the hall, and only Angantyr is credited with the
troll-like bellowing. Indeed one feels throughout the Sumbø
version a more clearly defined hostility to Angantyr on the
part of the balladist, whereas the Westmanhavn version is
more detached in its attitude.

THE DANISH BALLAD OF ANGELFYR
AND HELMER

1. *Offue he dwelt in Uthiss-kier*, so MS. A. MS. B has
"*Alff....Odderskier.*" MS. C. has "*Ulff...Oderskier.*" MS. D
has "*Alff...Odderskiær.*" Axel Olrik, however, in the version
which he prints in *Danske Folkeviser i Udvalg*, p. 105 f. has
"Alf...Odderskær." He explains (Introduction, p. 78) Alf to
be 'a combination of Arngrim the father of the berserks and
Hjalmar's foster-brother Örvarodd.'

7. *Gold shone on his hand.* The phrase is not quite clear. It
may possibly refer to some personal ornament, but in view
of the following line, would seem more probably to indicate
that Angelfyr offered money to the King of Upsala.

11. *He is half a troll,* So A, which is in accordance with
Angelfyr's ancestry as told in the *Saga of Hervör and Heithrek*,
ch. 1. B and D, however, like the Faroese, have 'He is so
vile a troll.' A gives little sense, considering the second half
of the verse, and the whole becomes a meaningless formula in
all the versions in which Angantyr and Hjalmar are described
as brothers.

18. *Whom he himself will have.* Possibly *han*, 'he,' is a
misprint for *hón*, 'she,' which is what we should expect.
Cf. the *Saga of Hervör and Heithrek*, ch. 3. One hardly
expects a cynical touch like this in an authentic ballad. But
the whole of the latter part of B may be a later version than
the original.

THE FAROESE BALLAD OF ARNGRIM'S SONS

Refrain. I have adopted the refrain given in Hammershaimb's version of the Ballad, taken down on Sandø in 1848
and published in the *Antiq. Tídss.*, 1849–1851, rather than
Svabo's version which he afterwards adopted, but which is
very obscure and possibly corrupt.

2. *Bjarnaland,* so sing the Faroese according to both Svabo and Hammershaimb. By *Bjarnaland* they mean Norway. Contrast, however, the *Saga of Hervör and Heithrek,* ch. 2, where we are distinctly told that Angantyr's mother was Eyfura who had been carried off by Arngrim from *Bjarmaland* (i.e. the land of the Perms) where her father was king. See also the note on this passage. The Faroese have no doubt confused the unfamiliar name with one more familiar to themselves.

3. *Beneath oak trees live they*—a common ballad formula with no real significance. It is interesting, however, as a touch indicating the literary origin of this and other stories told in the Faroese ballads. As has been remarked (see p. 247 above) there are no trees on the Faroes. On the other hand farm houses in Scandinavian lands stand frequently beneath the shadow of a large oak. For a discussion of this subject, see Chadwick, *Cult of Othin* (Cambridge, 1899), p. 72 ff. Compare the Scottish Ballad of *Rose the Red and White Lily,* v. 38:

> Then out and spak' the King again,
> Says, "Bonny boy, tell to me
> Who lives into yon bigly bow'r,
> Stands by yon green oak-tree?"

4. *Arngrim and the Earl's lady,* etc. So Svabo. In Hammershaimb's version (*Antiq. Tidss.* 1849–1851) she is described as the daughter of Angantyr.

7. *Better than fighting,* etc. The incident of a *boy* playing too roughly with his companions and being told by them to go and avenge his father instead of maltreating them is very widespread. Prof. Ker notes its occurrence (*On the History of the Ballads* 1100–1500, p. 194) in the Irish Romance of Maelduin, in four Norwegian, five Faroese, two or three Danish ballads, in a Literary History of the Arabs and in New Guinea.

8. *Water she cast,* etc. The passage is obscure. It is not clear if Hervik had actually been fighting with the 'lads,' so

that the cleansing of her armour was an actual necessity; or if she had only been playing rather roughly. *Leika* can mean both 'to play' and 'to fight'; and *leikvöllr* may mean both a 'playground' and a 'battlefield.' If Hervik had only been playing, the throwing of the water on the armour was possibly a rite performed before undertaking vengeance.

9. *Die on straw.* To 'die on straw' is the regular idiom in Faroese and Icelandic for to 'die in one's bed,' of old age or sickness, as opposed to death by the sword.

10. *Isan's Grove.* Hammershaimb suggests that by *Isan's Land* here and in vv. 20 and 21 below the Faroese mean *Samsø.* On the other hand there was a forest in Holstein in ancient times called *Isarnho,* and some such name may possibly be preserved here. There was a King *Isung* mentioned in the Danish Ballad *De vare syv og syvsindstyve,* as an opponent of King *Didrik;* but it is improbable that his land is here indicated.

13. *She drew a shirt from out the chest,* etc.—a common ballad motif. A verse almost identical with this is to be found in the *Kvæði of Regin the Smith,* v. 47.

14. *Up then rose Hervik,* etc. vv. 14, 15, 16 and 20 are identical with vv. 12–16 (inclusive) of *Olufu Kvæði,* the only change being that 'Hugin the King' takes the place of 'Hervik the Earl's daughter.' They are practically identical too with the *Kvæði of the Jómsvíkingar,* vv. 6–8 (inclusive). Cf. also *Sjurðar Kvæði* (III, *Högna Táttur,* vv. 46–49), and *Ragnarlikkja,* vv. 40–48.

20. *Striped gold on a scarlet ground.* The text has *Gull við reyðan brand,* which is probably a mishearing of the line *Gull við reyðan rand* ('with a gold stripe on a red ground'). Verse 39 of *Brúsajökils Kvæði* (which is otherwise identical with the above) gives in the second line *Gull við ráum brann* ('gold blazed on the yardarms'). In Hammershaimb's version of our ballad, vv. 10, 72, the line is *Gulli vovin við rand* ('woven with gold in stripes'), as also in v. 22 of the *Kvæði of Ormar Torolvsson.* The line also occurs in the form *Gull við vágum rann* ('the margin of the ship was gold down to

where it touched the waves'). This is no doubt corrupt, but it is difficult to conjecture as to which of all the variants was the original form of the line.

23. *Cast she down her anchor*, etc. vv. 23, 24 are the almost invariable formula for the landing in the Faroese ballads. They are practically identical with v. 46 of *Olufu Kvæði* and vv. 24, 25 of the *Kvæði of Ormar Torolvsson*. Cf. also *Sigmundar Kvæði*, v. 32; *Brúsajökils Kvæði*, v. 41 and the *Kvæði of Alvur Kongur*, vv. 24–26 and *Sjurðar Kvæði* (*Högna Táttur*, vv. 71–73).

25. *Herd and fee*. Either the word *jæge* or the word *fæ* seems to have an unusual sense here.

28. *Though quake now fell and fold*. The original (*kyk gekk jörð á fold*) is not clear. I have merely adopted Grundtvig's translation of Hammershaimb's early text in the *Antiq. Tíðss* 1849–1851. The 1855 ed. substitutes *hon* for *jörð* which is better.

35. *All in the middle*, etc. There is obviously a lacuna or transference of some kind here. For this and the following verses, cf. *Olufu Kvæði*, vv. 26, 27, which are identical except the names. Indeed it is a common formula in the Faroese and Danish Ballads, and occurs in the *Kvæði of Ormar Torolvsson*, v. 26; and the *Kvæði of Alvur Kongur*, v. 33.

36. *A hundred men and five*—a stock number in the Faroese ballads. Cf. the *Kvæði of Ormar Torolvsson*, v. 27, where we are also told that the King sat at the board 'with a hundred men and five.' Cf. also *Olufu Kvæði*, v. 27.

37. *Mead or wine*, etc. Cf. *Sjurðar Kvæði* (III, *Högna Táttur*, v. 181).

52. Perhaps we should here again assume a lacuna or transposition.

Uppland is the old name for the modern province of Upsala in Sweden.

60. *Her cheeks they are as red and white*, etc. Cf. the *Kvæði of Finnur hin Fríði*, v. 18. Cf. also the old Celtic romance of the *Fate of the Sons of Usna*: "I should like," said Deirdre,

THE FAROESE GATU RIMA 253

"that he who is to be my husband should have these three colours: his hair as black as the raven: his cheeks red as the blood: his skin like the snow" (Joyce's translation). Cf. also Grimm's story of *Little Snowdrop*.

68. *Forth then when his frigate,* etc. vv. 68–84 are found in almost identical form in *Olufu Kvæði,* vv. 22–35.

69. *Angantyr was the first to light,* etc. A common ballad formula, both Faroese and Danish.

88. *I would not that lady Ingibjörg hear,* etc. Lit. "the lady Ingibjörg will learn that I fled." There is a suppressed condition. "If I let you fight, the lady Ingibjörg would learn, etc." Hammershaimb's text (*Antiq. Tídss.*) v. 37, has a negative and no condition: "The lady Ingibjörg shall not learn," etc.

97. *O Hjalmar, give me now a drink.* This incident appears to be taken from *Gunnlaugs Saga,* ch. 12.

THE FAROESE GATU RIMA

9. *Thunder is the red drum.* Probably *reyða* ('red') is a printer's error for *reiða* ('angry'), though the same form occurs also in the version of the ballad published in the *Antiquarisk Tídsskrift.* In v. 16, however, we find *skarið* whereas in v. 17 the word is written *skarðið,* the form used in both verses in *Antiq. Tídss.,* and the two words are obviously identical in both verses. Moreover in v. 21 *einir* ('own,' 'single') which gives little sense, is surely an error for *eingir* ('no,' adj.) as in vv. 11, 17, 19. The negative is also found in v. 21 in the version in the *Antiq. Tídss.,* in the form *ei,* 'they have *not* fathers or mothers.' Indeed the entire ballad would seem to be somewhat carelessly printed in *Færöiske Kvæðer.*

HILDINA

5. *St Magnus,* Earl of Orkney, 1108 to 1116. A cathedral was built at Kirkwall in his honour by one of his successors, Earl Ronald.

EDITIONS OF TEXTS USED FOR TRANSLATIONS

PART I

Fornaldar Sögur Norðrlanda, ed. by C. C. Rafn, published at Copenhagen, 1829.

Fornaldar Sögur Norðrlanda, ed. by Valdimar Ásmundarson, published by Sigurður Kristjánsson, Reykjavík, 1891–1911.

Die Prosaische Edda im Auszuge nebst Völsungasaga und Nornagestsþáttr, ed. with introduction and glossary by Ernst Wilken, Paderborn, 1877. 2nd ed., 1912.

Sagaen om Hervar ok Kong Heiðrek, ed. by N. N. Petersen and published (together with a Danish translation by G. Thorarensen), by the Norse Literature Society, Copenhagen, 1847.

PART II

Færöiske Kvæðer henhørende til Hervarar Saga, published by V. U. Hammershaimb in the *Antiquarisk Tidsskrift*, 1849–1851, Copenhagen, 1852.

Færöiske Kvæðer, published by V. U. Hammershaimb at Copenhagen, Part I, 1851; Part II, 1855.

Danmarks Gamle Folkeviser, Vol. I, collected and edited by Svend Grundtvig, 1853.

Griplur, published in *Rímnasafn*, edited by Finnur Jónsson, Copenhagen, 1905–1912, p. 351 ff.

NOTE: TRANSLATIONS

The following is a list of English translations of works referred to in the notes of the present volume. It is not in the nature of a bibliography; but for the convenience of English readers, reference has been given, whenever English translations are accessible, to the translations in preference to the original work.

Corpus Poeticum Boreale, 'The Poetry of the Old Northern Tongue from the earliest times to the Thirteenth Century,' 2 Vols., Vigfússon and Powell, Oxford, 1883.

Five Pieces of Runic Poetry, including *Hervör and Angantyr*, translated into prose by Bishop Percy, 1763.

Hickes's Thesaurus, including *Hervör and Angantyr*, translated into prose, Oxford, 1705.

The Elder or Poetic Edda, Part I, *The Mythological Poems*, translated and edited by Olive Bray; printed for the Viking Club, 1908.

The Edda of Sæmund, translated by B. Thorpe, published by Trübner and Co., London, 1866.

The Prose Edda, translated by A. G. Brodeur, New York, 1916.

Saxo Grammaticus, *Danish History*, Books I–IX, translated from the Latin by Professor Elton; published by D. Nutt, 1894 (the numbers in the notes refer to the pages of the translation, and not to the original Latin).

The Heimskringla, translated by W. Morris and E. Magnússon; published by B. Quaritch in *The Saga Library*, 1889.

The Saga of King Olaf Tryggwason, translated by J. Sephton and published by D. Nutt in *The Northern Library*, London 1895 (different from *The Story of Olaf Tryggvison* contained in the *Heimskringla*).

Islands Landnámabók—'The Book of the Settlement of Iceland,' translated by T. Ellwood and published at Kendal, 1898.

The Story of Egill Skallagrímsson, translated by W. C. Green, published by Elliot Stock, 1893.

Grettissaga—The Story of Grettir the Strong, translated by E. Magnússon and W. Morris, published by Longmans, Green and Co. (new edition), 1900. Also translated by G. A. Hight in Dent's *Everyman* Series.

Brennu Njálssaga—The Story of Burnt Njal, translated by G. W. Dasent; published by Edmonston and Douglas, Edinburgh, 1861; republished by Dent in the *Everyman* Series.

Three Northern Love Stories and other tales, translated by E. Magnússon and W. Morris. 2nd ed. 1901.

Völsunga Saga—The Story of Sigurth the Völsung, translated by W. Morris and E. Magnússon; published by the 'Walter Scott' Publishing Co. Ltd., London and Felling-on-Tyne.

The Nibelungenlied—The Lay of the Nibelung Men, translated into verse by Arthur S. Way; published at the Cambridge University Press, 1911. Also *The Lay of the Nibelungs*, translated into prose by Alice Horton, and edited by Edward Bell; published by George Bell and Sons, London, 1898. Also *The Fall of the Nibelungs*, translated by M. Armour in Dent's *Everyman* Series.

A further list of English translations of sagas not referred to in this book will be found in Craigie's *Icelandic Sagas*, ch. VII, p. 110. A list of foreign translations, especially translations into the various Teutonic languages, will be found in *Islandica*, issued by the Cornell University Library, Vol. V, compiled by Halldór Hermansson, 1912, pp. 3–7 (general) and *passim*.

For EU product safety concerns, contact us at Calle de José Abascal, 56–1°,
28003 Madrid, Spain or eugpsr@cambridge.org.

 www.ingramcontent.com/pod-product-compliance
Ingram Content Group UK Ltd.
Pitfield, Milton Keynes, MK11 3LW, UK
UKHW012330130625
459647UK00009B/184